Across the Spectrum

A journey towards understanding and supporting individuals with autism

Francine Brower and
Keith MacKenzie Cox

BLOOMSBURY EDUCATION
LONDON OXFORD NEW YORK NEW DELHI SYDNEY

BLOOMSBURY EDUCATION
Bloomsbury Publishing Plc
50 Bedford Square, London, WC1B 3DP, UK
29 Earlsfort Terrace, Dublin 2, Ireland

BLOOMSBURY, BLOOMSBURY EDUCATION and the Diana logo are trademarks of
Bloomsbury Publishing Plc

A catalogue record for this book is available from the British Library

ISBN: PB: 978-1-4729-8452-4; ePDF: 978-1-4729-8454-8; ePub: 978-1-4729-8453-1

2 4 6 8 10 9 7 5 3 1 (paperback)

Typeset by Newgen KnowledgeWorks Pvt. Ltd., Chennai, India
Printed and bound in the UK by CPI Group UK Ltd, Croydon CR0 4YY

MIX
Paper from
responsible sources
FSC® C013604
FSC
www.fsc.org

To find out more about our authors and books visit www.bloomsbury.com
and sign up for our newsletters

Contents

Acknowledgements

We would be remiss if we did not take this opportunity to recognise the contribution of our families as we applied ourselves to writing this book during the added stress of lockdown, isolation, children at home, concerns for extended families, disruption in routine and all that working from home brings. New lessons in patience have been ongoing. Thank you!

Over many years, we have had the privilege of working in different educational environments and having involvement in a variety of settings supporting individuals with autism from early childhood to adulthood. The examples in this book are taken from these settings, where the commitment of staff, the contribution of parents and the diversity of the children, young people and adults shine a light on the spectrum of autism.

We would like to thank our editor, Hannah Marston, for her encouragement and suggestions as the book progressed.

Our careers have been enriched by our individual and shared experiences but perhaps most influenced by our years together in Inscape House Salford (formerly a school of the Boys' and Girls' Welfare Society and now The Together Trust), where strong bonds were forged with colleagues, pupils and families. Their contribution in trying to unravel the unique challenges, asking hard questions and seeking answers was at the heart of the ethos of the school. Through a commitment to problem-solving and mutual determination to meet individual needs, the team shared ideas, frustrations and celebrations.

And, finally, thank you to our illustrators, Anna and Leon Brower, for being creative on our behalf!

Keith and Francine

Introduction

Collaborating to write this book has been both a positive and a challenging experience. Each of the authors has been committed to working with individuals with autism and their families for over a quarter of a century. We have learned so much from the unique and diverse children and young people we have supported, as well as from their families and carers. The privilege of working with a wide range of professionals has enabled robust discussion and mutual learning.

This book is being written in 2020, as the world struggles to keep COVID-19 from decimating countries on every continent. We write from our homes, with meetings enabled through technology. Communication continues but face-to-face socialisation is impossible. Across the globe, households are in lockdown and coping with the 24/7 needs of their children, separation from friends and loved ones, and loss of life, without being able to provide comfort. For parents and carers with autistic children, the changes in routine and the unpredictable nature of daily living is a constant challenge. Whatever normal was may never be the same again. Many teachers and care workers are on the front line helping to support the most vulnerable and keep them safe. We clap for them; we applaud the commitment that they demonstrate.

This book is not intended to be a textbook or a theoretical analysis of autism but rather a reflection of the diversity that is seen across the autism spectrum. The examples given in the book are our way of shining a light on the diverse presentations that we have encountered. All names have been changed and when scenarios make you smile, we are not in any way laughing at our children and young people. Rather, we are trying to give a true picture of the day-by-day situations that arise in the pursuit of attempting to understand and support individuals on the autism spectrum and their families and carers. Through this book we are exploring together, describing, seeking reasons that are not always found. We consider strategies and interventions that are used widely but we do not pretend to seek or advocate 'cures'. Accepting each individual and enabling each to become the best they can be, living lives that are healthy and fulfilling, is the ultimate goal. We believe that individuals with autism, young and old, should not just be enabled to *cope* but must be given the opportunity to **thrive**.

Autism is a relatively new disorder, being first named and identified in the middle of the last century by Leo Kanner and Hans Asperger. Working separately, on different continents, with small groups of children who presented as aloof, alone, self-absorbed and markedly different in their interactions, the similarities and diversities were recognised. Eugen Bleuler coined the term 'autism' in the early part of the 20th century to describe the social withdrawal that is sometimes seen in schizophrenia, coming from the Greek word *autos*, meaning self. Over the past 70-plus years since Leo Kanner and Hans Asperger identified this separate and idiosyncratic group, the prevalence and identification of autism have grown exponentially. While statistics on prevalence vary across countries, the current figure in the UK is more than one in 100 (UK Parliament, 2020). Recognising that autism is a lifelong developmental disability and that individuals of all ages are affected, we are very conscious of the need for community awareness, appropriate support and the right services to be provided for individuals and their extended families and friends.

Autism in all its forms affects essential human behaviours, including communication, social interaction, the ability to communicate ideas and feelings, restricted interests and repetitive behaviours. Many people with autism also experience sensory issues that have an impact on their ability to cope. Each chapter of this book addresses one of these issues, as well as presentations of behaviour, and the current climate with respect to diagnosis, support and community integration, and it finishes with an overview of the varied experiences and needs of families and carers. Through examples of individuals who represent the spectrum, we strive to broaden the reader's understanding and draw awareness of the challenges and possibilities for enriching lives.

As you read this book, you will become aware that, while each chapter highlights a different topic, there is an inevitable overlap. It is, for example, impossible to discuss communication without touching on socialisation. Anxiety sparked by issues of inflexibility and unanticipated change or because of sensory overload may trigger behaviours that others find challenging. By recognising the interweaving of these areas, you will become more alert to the confusion faced by autistic individuals and, hopefully, heighten your own understanding and feel inspired to persevere creatively in your support.

The DSM-5 (*Diagnostic and Statistical Manual of Mental Disorders*) notes that autism is sometimes referred to as an umbrella term for a wide spectrum of disorders. Each autism spectrum disorder is unique in its pattern of challenges and areas of relative strengths. Throughout this book, a range of terms are used interchangeably, including autism, autistic, autism spectrum disorder, ASD and on the spectrum.

Further areas that present challenges include 'executive function', which affects organisation, planning, paying attention, short-term memory and multitasking.

'Central coherence' is also explored, referring to the difficulty in seeing the bigger picture or recognising the context of a situation.

You will read the term *neurotypical* throughout the book. This is a relatively new term that's used to describe individuals of typical developmental, intellectual and cognitive abilities, assuming that this is the 'general public'. Some assume that the neurotypical perception of the world is the only right one. We would disagree with this. Individuals on the autism spectrum are not *less than* but *different from*. Adaptations need to be made by society to understand, embrace and celebrate diversity.

Underpinning our commitment to autism is a belief that the *ethos* of any organisation or establishment must be fit for purpose to offer opportunities for success. Ethos refers to the underlying beliefs and character that permeate the environment, set the tone and create the atmosphere. This should include:

- recognising and attempting to understand each individual
- treating everyone with dignity and respect
- upholding high expectations
- looking for creative solutions rather than problems
- building on strengths rather than emphasising weaknesses
- offering a consistent approach
- making reasonable adjustments to the environment and resources.

We hope that the picture of autism, its diversity and its similarities, will help the reader to have a new appreciation of this wonderfully unique group of individuals. Too often, we expect the person on the autism spectrum to do the changing. We encourage you to consider the sentiment expressed by Temple Grandin on 'The Best Life for Animals' in 2009: 'You can't make me into something that I'm not... You've got to meet halfway.' We long for a society that embraces and supports the contribution of every member and celebrates the contribution that each can make.

1 Communication: So much more than words

Communication is one of the key challenges faced by individuals on the autism spectrum. Indeed, the 'failure' to develop communication can be an early indicator of autism. The presentation of this issue is from non-verbal to highly verbal and many, many communicative intents can be missed if the listener is not in tune with what is being attempted by the other person. This chapter addresses this diversity, providing examples of the challenges that are faced, the hurdles that need to be overcome and the ways in which understanding and creative support can be offered to enable progress. It recognises the essential role that is played by communication partners, be those family members, peers, education, support or therapy staff. A myriad of examples will shine a light on the confusing and often misunderstood journey to navigate communication.

As you read this chapter, there are some important points to bear in mind.

- Verbal communication is only one aspect of communication – it is a combination of body language, facial expression, gesture, context and tone of voice.

- Language is composed of **receptive language**, which is understanding words, sentences and the meaning of what is being said, and **expressive language**, which is the communication of feelings, wants and needs to a communication partner.

- Unlike a 'typically' developing child, who quickly learns to respond to faces and to develop an awareness of eye contact and facial expression, a child with autism typically misses the reciprocal nature of communication and the importance of the two-way process.

Communication is one of the ways in which we interact with others. Most of us take this for granted, whether it be through speech, facial expression, gesture, print or tone of voice.

Preverbal and non-verbal individuals

The terms non-verbal and preverbal, although similar, have clear distinctions. Generally, preverbal refers to individuals who express themselves through vocalisations and gesture rather than through the use of words. There is an expectation that a preverbal child will gradually develop emerging verbal communication. Non-verbal individuals may use vocalisations but without words or meaningful speech. Some individuals on the autistic spectrum remain non-verbal throughout their lives. Individuals are assessed and supported to develop appropriate communication systems to make their needs known and to enhance quality of life.

Craig, at eight years of age, was preverbal. His communication was at a very early stage of development. He showed little or no interest in others around him. He would, on occasion, come and take someone's hand to attempt to get an object that was out of his reach.

The term 'non-verbal' could perhaps seem to be pejorative without meaning to be. It suggests that Craig had actively decided not to verbalise, and while selective mutism is an area that will be discussed further on in this chapter, it does not describe Craig or his communication. In trying to communicate with a person who is 'stuck' in the preverbal stage, the key is often to find a shared language to help the person see and understand that there is a purpose behind their communicative intent. Craig loved the Disney classics and would frequently make vocalisations (or 'babble') of the key tunes and sounds. Craig struggled to enter our world but this special interest gave us a door into his. Using Craig's interest in Disney, particularly Winnie the Pooh, allowed us to develop the very early fundamentals of communication. By echoing Craig's vocalisations back to him, he was learning to give very brief attention to another person; by sharing space and time with Craig in a non-pressured, very low-demand way, his attention was extended.

Intensive interaction

For those who struggle with communication, specific approaches are often employed. One of these is intensive interaction, which has as its underlying principle the interactions used by adults with babies in their first year. The sensitive and intuitive practitioner follows the child's lead. The adult has to be relaxed, non-directive and responsive to the child's vocalisations, their actions and any perceived attempt at an interaction. Sessions can be very intense and they need to be frequent, but they can be immensely rewarding, fun-filled and enjoyable to both parties. Nabil is an example of a preverbal child who occasionally played with sounds and volume but did not use spoken language and struggled to make his needs known. In a quiet, distraction-free area, he had individual sessions of intensive interaction using bubbles. With a lead-in of 'Ready, steady [long pause], go', bubbles filled the air and the space was filled with giggles. Over time, with the routine of this session, the 'ready, steady' prompt was completed by Nabil enthusiastically shouting, 'Go!' This further led Nabil to initiating the entire phrase, and before long, he began to request 'More'.

Tip

Intensive interaction can be used in a very meaningful and productive way throughout the day, at home, in school and in the community. Examples abound: at playtime on the veranda, with two members of staff on their knees at eye level with individual children; a member of staff on the car mat close to a child and another making letters or marks together on a large sheet of paper; or a mum who uses the walk to and from school to imitate her daughter's vocalisations and playfully draw her into the wonders of the environment.

Communication through music

Another intervention is communication through music. This uses songs, games and musical 'conversations' to engage pupils in social interaction. In many ways it replicates the early interventions with infants through rhymes, echoing, early babble and attempts at communication. Learning through these shared experiences promotes the development of communication skills, such as eye contact, turn-taking, imitation, shared attention and initiating interaction, at a level appropriate to the individual's needs. Craig, described above, showed how much he loved these sessions by dancing, twirling and giving intense hugs. More importantly, these sessions were showing his family a way into Craig's world, and their relationship was deepening and strengthening.

Music often draws people in. Good morning sessions in schools use music as a time to gather. Melissa wandered around the classroom and avoided sitting in the group circle and participating with her peers. Her teacher did not pressure her to

Figure 1.1 *A music choice board*

come but would gently pat the chair set out for her and say her name. Over time, Melissa drew closer and closer when the music began. Well-chosen songs were part of the routine and the children were given objects to hold that reflected the theme: laminated frogs for 'Five Little Speckled Frogs' and rubber ducks for 'Five Little Ducks Swam Away'. The objects were placed on the empty chair. Melissa began to pick them up and hold them. Slowly but surely, she joined the group with full participation.

It is not uncommon for staff to give an instruction through a tune, and music is commonly used to draw attention to transition time in class. This was beautifully done in one setting, where the tidy-up music to get ready for hand-washing and lunch was 'Food, Glorious Food' – very effective! Music further links to communication when opportunities for choosing the song are given. A choice board with objects or symbols enables children to express what they want.

Attention Autism

In recent years, an intervention called 'Attention Autism' has been developed by Gina Davies, a specialist speech and language therapist, to help parents and professionals give their child with autism an irresistible invitation to learn by using fantastic activities and having a really good time while doing so. This approach provides the child with an experience worth communicating about. It has been a privilege to observe sessions where children were so captivated and awe-inspired that they watched intently, waited expectantly and responded with enthusiasm. In one session, a balloon was used by the teacher and each time one of the children made a comment, the balloon was blown up just a little bit more. Words like 'big', 'bigger', 'more', 'giant' and 'gigantic' prompted the blowing up of the balloon, which was then whizzed around the classroom like a firework. The delight of every child was shown in facial expressions and cheers. The skills being developed – waiting, attention, anticipation, shared interest, turn-taking and responding – all support the development of communication. The exaggerated responses and facial expressions of staff members engendered interest from the pupils.

Commentary

Another useful tool to encourage vocabulary and language development is through commentary. This is simply commenting on what is happening in any context and helping to link vocabulary to actions and emotions. For example, when a facial expression shows sadness, say, 'You are sad' and reflect that in your own face or show a photo or symbol that displays the emotion. Working with Ellie as she first came to the Reception class was a challenge. Her language was limited to a very loud 'NO!' and some 'expletive deleted' words. A favourite activity was sand and water play, and as she played, comments were quietly added: 'Ellie is pouring/sifting/digging', etc. Before long, she was telling us that she was pouring or sifting or digging. Her vocabulary increased by leaps and bounds. Suggesting a similar approach to her mother was a way of opening up Ellie's world; as she added words to her vocabulary every day, nature and the local community became 'known' to her, as she absorbed the commentary offered to her.

The presentation of autism in verbal communication

Borrowed language

It is often difficult to explain why individuals with autism develop communication in the way in which they do. Each individual is unique and it follows that their response and timing will also be unique. Take Joe, for example, who came into school as a bright and often very contented, bouncy, nursery-aged pupil. In the pre-entry discussions and meetings, it was clear that his parents had identified very early on that Joe was markedly different from his older brother in hitting his developmental milestones. Joe was a very physically able baby: he crawled, climbed and walked from a very early age – in fact, much earlier than his brother. Other key areas, however, were very different. He was very slow to develop speech and they had concerns that Joe may, in fact, be deaf, as he didn't react to his name and did not respond to noises such as planes, sirens, etc. Although he loved television and had very particular favourites, his play was solitary and very different from his older brother's. Joe's parents had, from a very early age, sought the support, advice and guidance from the local Child Development Team, and at 38 months Joe received a diagnosis of autism.

When Joe joined school in September, he had some ability to make his needs known: he could ask for a drink or a snack using one-word utterances or use a staff member as a tool to get what he wanted. The first term was positive; he settled well and quickly adapted to the routine and structure of the class. The first day back after the Christmas break, Joe bounded in speaking in a very loud American accent and addressed his teacher as Mr Ratburn (readers of a certain age will know exactly what Joe had been watching!). Joe had developed his speech and communication through watching TV and, in particular, *Arthur's Teacher Trouble* (adapted from the book by Marc Brown, 1986). Once Joe realised that speaking could get things he wanted, he made full use of this – he continued to have significant difficulties with social communication, but we now had a shared language.

Yes, this may seem shocking and unusual and yet it is not uncommon. Borrowed language from television, books and films is often reported. Dwight loved the *Thomas the Tank Engine* books and all that went with them. He struggled to find conventional vocabulary but, when he was struggling with an activity, he would pound the desk and declare, 'There's trouble in the shed.' We quickly realised that this was his way of asking for help. Similarly, when in the community, he would comment that, 'The fat controller says the signal is down', indicating that the traffic light had turned red. Although we had to interpret the phrases, they made very good sense and served as functional communication.

A very creative use of borrowed language was when a student took objection to being observed at work and asked, 'What are you looking at, you gender-confused old woman?' The calm response was to agree about being an old woman but to deny the other! The latter part of the comment was apparently taken from a well-known film that was regularly enjoyed by the student.

It is also interesting that accents are adopted, like Joe above. Ellis spoke in a very posh accent and we assumed that that was a very natural part of his family setting. When his parents, who spoke in a broad Mancunian accent, visited school, they explained that they had been listening to the radio one day when the Queen was speaking. From that moment on, Ellis imitated her and stood out among his peers.

Members of staff who hail from different parts of the world often hear their own accents coming back to them when working with a child, as well as having parents comment on their child imitating the accents at home! Why does this occur? Perhaps it is related to the lack of inhibition of caring what others think and choosing to be whatever they want. We may be able to learn from that!

Echolalia

In addition to borrowed language, 'echolalia' is not unusual as language used by individuals with autism. It is the repetition of 'chunks' of language, often repeating what has been said by another person. When greeting someone we often say 'good morning', and if the response is 'good morning' in return, we accept this as correct. If, however, you said, 'Good morning, Mary' and Mary responded with 'Good morning, Mary', she would merely be echoing your words. Children with emerging communication can use echolalia to communicate feelings or emotions. Billy would use, 'That's it, you're fired' to convey anxiety or when he was uncertain – the phrase had come from a favourite reading book. The echolalia allowed us to help him to develop a more readily accessible and understandable phrase. Billy repeating the phrase, 'That's it, you're fired' over and over was a useful barometer of his level of anxiety and gave us an opportunity to reduce his arousal.

The first time I (Francine) encountered Danny, I was supporting his group at lunchtime. He had finished his lunch and said 'yogurt', indicating that he wanted more. I replied, 'Sorry, no more yogurt.' For years, every time he saw me he said, 'No more yogurt.' One day, as I passed him in the playground, he looked up, smiled and said, 'Hello, Francine.' I was stunned. Why did he choose that day to change his greeting to me? What had changed? I will never know. Several years later when I visited the school where he remained a student, he greeted me warmly and said, 'I used to know you, didn't I, Francine?' Great communication development!

Delayed echolalia and repeating chunks of language out of context need to be very carefully considered and assessed. Mario frequently repeated 'chunks' of news reports. He would make attempts at social interaction with adults – always adults – by repeating almost word for word parts of the previous day's news. The problem was that it was a mechanical exercise; there was very little comprehension of the meaning of what Mario was recounting, and therefore developing conversation was very difficult. Mario was desperate to have social interactions with adults and his conversational skills were addressed through participation in small social skills groups with peers.

Delayed echolalia can be very confusing for the listener, as the context of the language is often unknown. Alice would occasionally utter a sentence that could be interpreted – for example, 'I'm sorry Alice, I can't let you do that', said in a perfect imitation of her mother's voice. Paul gave a glimpse into life at home when he uttered, 'You get that arse of yours upstairs', particularly when he was feeling stressed.

Repetitive questioning

Repetitive questioning is another way in which verbalisation sometimes conveys anxiety or excitement. It is important to recognise that this is an attempt to communicate and we should be attuned to this. There are times when reassurance is being sought, such as 'Where is mum?' repeated over and over again. Continuing to provide the answer 'Mum is at home' can become irritating, but turning it around to ask, 'Can you tell me where your mum is?' can help to reassure.

Tip

Sometimes, explaining that the question can be asked three times and then making it clear that questions are finished can reduce the distraction that this causes.

Tools to support communication

Picture Exchange Communication System®

The 'Picture Exchange Communication System' (PECS)® has been used to support the development of communication for many years. It is a system that can allow those who have a very limited voice to make themselves heard and is used by all ages, all cognitive abilities and a wide range of communication challenges. It is based on prompting and reinforcement and is clearly presented in stages, for which training is widely available. Although often used for snacks and meals, there is a wealth of daily opportunities to encourage the user to express preferences and opinions, and when used at its best, it opens up the world of communication for those who do not use speech. Although initially time-intensive, the commitment is well worthwhile when the frustration of being unable to make one's voice heard becomes a thing of the past.

In the early stages, the child will 'exchange' a single picture (commonly a photo of a favourite toy, etc.) for the object on the picture; a very simple exchange has taken place, the child has been rewarded and, over time, the goal is that they will come to the realisation that communication is a positive experience. As the child or young person moves through the stages, requests become gradually more complex and adjectives are added: 'I would like the red car' or 'I would like the green apple'. An excellent example is when Stewart selected the symbol for a biscuit at snack time. The biscuit tin was offered to him and he pushed it away. He tried again and the teacher offered him the tin again. He pushed it away. He then looked through his PECS® book, found the colour brown and offered the two cards, brown and biscuit. Yes, he wanted a chocolate biscuit. Very clear communication! Now there was a problem – he needed to be rewarded but there were no chocolate biscuits in the tin. This was easily resolved as a member of staff went in search of one and successfully presented this young PECS® user with what he had chosen. Great motivation for the future!

A very dedicated teacher realised that Anna, who found her 'voice' through PECS®, was becoming bored with the symbols and pictures as she developed the ability to read. She continued to be non-verbal and the decision was made to replace the symbols with words. She adapted to this very quickly and used printed words to make sentences to comment and request. The gift of reading and communication through the printed word was celebrated.

A further example highlights preparing for a group trip to the shops, with each child having a 'shopping list' card showing the choices made from photos on a display board. To avoid frustration, the choices were not limited to one symbol or photo of each item. After choosing, the item was attached to the individual shopping list. The list and money were then put into a bag – also chosen by each from a selection. In the shop, the children retrieved their own list to match to items on the shelves and handled the money independently. The staff in the shop exercised great patience in waiting for each pupil to match and find their desired shopping item, attach it to their PECS® strip of 'I want… please' and exchange this with the shopkeeper.

Tip

One of the features of PECS® is that it can be taken into the community and used successfully – children, young people and adults taking their PECS® books with them into cafés and shops to independently request or ask for items is a very rewarding activity. The school's local McDonald's® became very adept at responding to exchanged sentence strips!

Rewarding communication

It is always important to use your creativity to *entice* the individual with autism to communicate with others, to find a way to make communication a valuable and rewarding activity. If we offer an individual everything that they need, we reduce the need for communication. If we put some things out of reach or make them unavailable unless requested, we challenge the person to find a way to get the reward. This is sometimes accomplished by putting favoured items too high for the person to reach (safely, of course, to avoid dangerous climbing). Taking your hand to show you what is wanted *is* communicating. Using a symbol to exchange with you *is* communicating. Luke had favourite snacks in the bottom of the kitchen cupboard and helped himself to chocolate buttons and crisps at will. This was not particularly healthy but also meant that he had no need to communicate to be well satisfied. By moving these things to a top shelf with a choice board on the bottom cupboard, he learned to seek out a member of the family and communicate his needs.

Sometimes we miss the communication that an individual is desperately trying to show us. We need to be attuned to every gesture, utterance or signal that is made. In this way, the communication is rewarded and becomes recognised as worthwhile. For example, a teacher suggested that a pupil bounced on a therapy ball, knowing that he liked to do this. The pupil did so unenthusiastically and then touched a nearby drum. Realising that he wanted the drum, she offered it to him. She was alert to his communicative intent and he was rewarded. This situation may have been enhanced if the pupil had been introduced to PECS® or had a visual choice board to put him 'in charge' of his resources.

Tip

Choice-making activities within structured sessions are well established, but opportunities for pupils to make requests and needs known outside of these times increase independence.

Emma was frustrated and tried to make her teacher understand what she wanted. She just didn't get it. Emma held up her shoe and the teacher asked whether it was hurting her foot. No. She asked whether she needed help with her laces. No. Emma tried so hard to communicate that her teacher could see the wheels turning. She went to the cupboard, brought out the wet wipes and said, 'Clean!'

A new word, a clear message. Her determination resulted in clear communication that could have otherwise led to a difficult incident.

Social communication

Aloofness from others, a lack of interest in other people and being self-contained often limit social niceties such as greetings. We typically say hello and goodbye, we greet others and ask after their wellbeing. This is often a difficult concept for individuals with autism. Working with a class of secondary students, we tried hard to emphasise social communication and made some progress with greetings and farewells through putting written prompts on posters for when entering and leaving the room. Having visitors to the group always proved a challenge, as each member of the group had an opening gambit that followed the expected hello.

Victoria: *'Hello, do you like cats?'*
Michael: *'Hello, have you ever been to Basingstoke?'*
Basid: *'Hello, have you ever been to the USA?'*
Andrew: *'Hello, do you like Rab C. Nesbitt?'*

It was very difficult to understand what was behind some of the questions, and visitors were often challenged in how to answer! Victoria did not have a cat, Michael had never been to Basingstoke, Basid continued on if the answer was yes and began to list each state (he had to be limited to three) and Andrew did not understand why anyone did not love his favourite character. Each was attempting to connect and that was good. Some support in widening topics of conversation was addressed through social skills.

Tip

If you are learning to use your voice in situations that are extremely nerve-wracking, such as a school or classroom, you have to have courage. The environment is full of unpredictability and full of others who themselves make strange noises, unusual facial expressions and confusing gestures. Children can be particularly unpredictable, while adults tend to be more consistent in their responses. Perhaps this is why children with autism tend to gravitate towards adults. Lance described his peers as annoying and bothersome but thought that adults were worth talking to!

Selective mutism

For most of us, if we have just plucked up the courage to attempt to speak with someone and, for whatever reason, it didn't go to plan, we would most likely try again and persevere. For some, repairing the conversation is too difficult and is abandoned. They make the decision that to attempt to 'speak' in this setting is too much. *Selective mutism* is a severe anxiety disorder where a person is unable to speak in certain social situations, such as with classmates at school or to relatives they do not see very often. Selective mutism can very quickly become entrenched and be generalised across a range of 'social' settings, including home. Although this social anxiety disorder can be separate from autism, they are frequently comorbid. Rob had spoken when he was in his primary special school, but he lacked confidence and was generally a quiet boy. On moving up to secondary school, he simply stopped speaking; he would talk quite animatedly with his big sister at home but adults could not hear his voice. He had made this rule and he stuck to it rigidly up until he entered post-16. He was very keen on the idea of work experience, especially on the idea of cleaning or working in a shop. A support assistant who had worked with Rob when he would speak in primary school began working with him again. He would whisper to her. Over the next few months, Rob started to talk again – only in certain circumstances and with a select few. Eventually, however, when he was placed in work experience he flourished. Through giving time, acceptance, specific relaxation techniques and trust, Rob got his voice back. The anxiety that many children can feel in social situations and, to add to that, the demand to communicate verbally can be a challenge too far, and demands that we be alert, supportive and patient!

Misinterpretation

We take so much for granted when we are communicating. We use facial expression, gesture, body language and tone of voice without even giving it a thought. But if these incidentally learned actions are not recognised, much of what is being communicated is lost. This is often the case with individuals with autism. This can lead to misinterpretation, such as when a parent or teacher raises their voice to be heard and it is interpreted as anger with the individual. In a school context, Jayden saw a peer with an angry face in the toilet and misinterpreted the anger as aggression, pushing the other boy and running down the corridor screaming. The other child was upset because he had been given a detention but Jayden didn't have the skills to ask why he was upset or to walk away from the situation – it was all about him. Teaching the gaps, using role play, scenarios and photographs and attaching meaning to them, helps to navigate the journey of frustration.

Social inhibitor

When we communicate with others, we generally have a filter that helps us to know what is acceptable and polite. This does not mean that our thoughts always match up with what we say, but we stop ourselves from insulting and hurting the feelings of others. This filter is not always present with individuals on the autism spectrum and can create barriers in relationships and friendships. Families, friends and professionals learn very quickly not to take things personally if they are insulted. Strangers are not always so forgiving. The person is really calling a spade a spade, speaking the truth as they see it, without the awareness that what is being said is offensive and hurtful. When Emily told the teacher, in front of the class group, that she didn't like the spot on the teacher's face, it was not well received. Similarly, when a male visitor with a generous build came into a classroom as an observer, Aleena looked him up and down and said, 'Do you have a baby in that big tummy of yours?' The gentleman was red with embarrassment and ushered out of the class to receive an explanation for the question. Had he stayed longer, he would have heard Aleena turn her attention to a member of staff and ask, 'Do you have a baby in that little finger of yours?' This may have helped him to understand that the question was not a personal affront but a verbal train of thought.

Alex had been taking part in social skills groups and lots of work had been done on giving and receiving compliments; it was going so well until he approached a visitor to school with, 'I really like your yellow and brown teeth!' Developing a social inhibitor is extremely problematic – the visitor did indeed have teeth that were somewhat discoloured. Alex had not yet developed the ability to discriminate in his social interactions. He had the habit of telling an overweight member of staff that it was time that she lost some weight. In a supportive and sheltered environment like a school, Alex was understood and could learn from such comments – in the wider community, he may not have had such understanding responses!

Tip

It is so important to remember that when things do go wrong and when insults are given, finding ways to explain, support and create an understanding of why the comments cause upset is vitally important. One way in which we have addressed this is to use the diagram in Figure 1.2 or, better still, photos of the individual to personalise it.

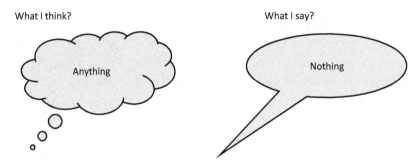

Figure 1.2 *What I think and what I say*

Special interests

The way in which we communicate has an impact on how we connect to others, and on the development of friendships and how relationships develop. For many verbal people on the autism spectrum, entering a conversation and being part of a social group is difficult to achieve. One young man in secondary school, Fahar, had developed a special interest in the bus timetables in the town where he lived. There is nothing inherently wrong with this at all. He did, however, use this as his only topic of conversation with his peers, and once he began to provide information for them they quickly lost interest. He was considered eccentric and found it very difficult to enter into the circle of teens. Listening to the arrival and departure times, bus numbers, destinations, etc. was not the kind of conversation in which his peers engaged. Once again, when an issue of this nature arises, it is so important to find a way to help the young person to recognise the reasons for others wandering away. Helping Fahar to find areas of *common* interest, identifying peers who will provide understanding and friendship, will help him to build bridges now and into the future.

Christopher was in a mainstream primary, and academically he was coping. However, he was finding it increasingly difficult to develop and maintain friendships. He was incredibly single-track in his conversations. He hadn't developed the conversational skills of turn-taking, taking account of the communication partner's interest levels or allowing the true to and fro of conversation. Christopher was having a series of monologues and it did not really dawn on him that there was no input from his peers. Mainstream primary schools tend to be more supportive and understanding but secondary school may not be. Christopher's special interest was *Dr Who* and this was used to help him to begin to develop some necessary conversational skills. In actual fact, there is a great deal of conversation within an episode of the sci-fi classic and this was used to help. Role play and, more specifically, re-enactment, were very useful tools, along with conversation cards and getting Christopher to relay messages and information throughout the school. Christopher did make significant progress; however, the intensity of the input and time off curriculum would not always be feasible in a secondary school setting.

Many highly verbal individuals with autism find it very difficult to enter into dialogue and to recognise the signs that their communication partner is bored. Teaching the subtle messages that help to engage with others is essential. By exaggerating yawning, facial expression, eye contact and body language through role play, these issues can be supported and enable people on the autism spectrum to have meaningful relationships if desired.

Processing time

We talk about the challenges that people on the autism spectrum face and yet there are many challenges that we as neurotypicals have in communicating appropriately with autistic individuals. One of these is understanding the importance of processing time. It can be vital to give an individual with autism time to process a verbal request. It requires a great deal of effort to translate a request for information or even a simple response. It can be very difficult to work out what the key words in a verbal sentence are – especially so if there are similes, idioms or a degree of ambiguity. Simplified language and a reasonable period of time to respond can make a positive impact. We often speak at pace and use a jumble of words that are just too numerous and too fast to follow. Allowing processing time, enabling messages to be received, is a skill to be learned. Consider this example: Jenny was brought to the headteacher's office for a reward sticker when she finished a new activity. Her teaching assistant accompanied her and she was shown a range of choices. Jenny examined them closely. The assistant immediately said, 'Pick one, Jenny', immediately followed by 'Choose one', followed by 'Which one do you want?' The headteacher indicated to the assistant to back away and slowly said, 'Jenny, pick a sticker.' Silence. Several seconds later she made a choice and gave a huge smile. As long as new words kept being offered and the key words changed, it was impossible for Jenny to follow the instructions.

> **Tip**
>
> Stop and think about how quickly you are speaking, the number of words you are using and the speed with which you change your delivery. Allow time for processing!

Communication

Written conversations

Another tool that can be used if the individual is literate is a written conversation. This ensures that there is processing time, with answers given when the person is ready. Jackson struggled to hold a conversation but had the ability to express himself in writing. The conversation went something like this:

Good morning, Jackson. How are you today?

> *I'm OK, are you OK?*

Yes I am. What did you do after school yesterday?

> *I played in the garden and watched telly.*

Is your family OK?

> *Mum has a cold.*

I'm sorry. I hope she is better soon.

> *Me too.*

Would you like to ask me any questions?

> *Are we going out today?*

Yes, we are. We have the minibus to use.

> *Good. I like that.*

It would have been impossible to have this conversation through speech, but by using the printed word, it went smoothly and without anxiety. Yes, it takes a bit of time but the rewards are well worth it. A school council meeting was observed where the student representatives responded in writing. As a result, valuable information was gleaned by the staff sponsor. Everyone was given a voice and felt valued.

People who have autism who write about living with the condition describe the difficulties that they can encounter with verbal communication. Donna Williams gives some insight into the problem of living in our world when she talks about her experiences in school in the quote on the next page.

> *'The biology teacher suggested that I use the calculator. I didn't know how. He tried to show me how it worked. When he asked me to work out a percentage of something, I tried to find the off button and gave up, furious and frustrated.'*
>
> *(Williams, 1998)*

The above quote highlights the difficulties in the translation from neurotypical speak into autism understanding. We often emphasise the importance of looking at the speaker, and generally we can filter out the non-verbal messages from the eyes, facial expression, changing tone and prosody. Lack of eye contact has been emphasised as a diagnostic criteria, and too much or not enough eye contact can make you stand out. Putting an emphasis on this adds a burden to the communicative process for many people with autism. We have learned from individuals on the spectrum that insisting on eye contact creates a distraction that inhibits listening to the message. This can be because of the attention being diverted to saliva on the lip, crooked teeth, the movement of the lips, etc. By allowing the person to look beyond or to the side, the sense that is being maximised is auditory. It is always worth bearing this in mind.

Visual support

It is recognised that most people with autism are visual learners. That is to say that they benefit from seeing things presented in a concrete way rather than purely through the spoken word. Perhaps many of you relate to this. Would you be lost without your diary? Do you always write a to-do list, a shopping list or a reminder for an appointment? There are many ways to communicate, reduce frustration and make the world a predictable place through visual supports. They provide a clear message that does not disappear into the ether like a spoken word. They include the use of symbols such as 'Wait' in Figure 1.3 and are so useful when in a queue or when taking turns. This simple message, with reassurance from the person supporting the young person, can reduce anxiety. A wealth of symbols to support life skills and to schedule activities enables structure to be seen and followed. But it is not just symbols; the visual must reflect the level of understanding of the individual. While some may need an actual concrete object to get the meaning, e.g. a mug to represent a drink or a roll of toilet tissue to represent the need for the toilet, others benefit from an elaborate weekly schedule or mobile phone app. So many low-tech visual supports can underpin communication – volume monitors, sand or electronic timers, photographs of choices to be made for dinner or beverages (we all rely on menus as our visual support when eating out),

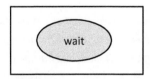

Figure 1.3 *Laminated lunchtime place mat with visual supports*

signage on doors and cupboards (where would we be if toilet doors didn't display symbols?), task lists, etc. A helpful example is the use of a laminated placemat for school lunch with the wait symbol on one side, turned over to reveal a template for plate, glass and cutlery when it is the child's time to join the queue. Life can be so confusing when things are unclear – let's make sure that we take every opportunity to communicate visually.

Technology

Of course, we live in the day of technology, and while low-tech works very well, the amazing opportunities for communication through mobile phone apps, talk pads, tablets, BIGmacks and a range of switches and voice output communication aids seem unlimited. Through technology, visual aids are made more accessible. Simon had a 'talk pad' and this included a photo of the residence where he lived, supporting transition from school at the end of the day. He also used this to indicate choices at snack time and for leisure time activities, as well as for morning greetings. Without it he was confused and insecure, but through its use Simon was given confidence and the opportunity to express himself.

Literal understanding

Literal understanding often causes confusion and sometimes embarrassment. In a school council meeting, the adult mentor emphasised wellbeing within the school. A discussion was held on how to support a new student entering the school, with the young people committing to help show him around, sit with him at breaks and try to initiate conversation. The staff member asked whether anyone wanted to 'be in charge of him' and a student responded, 'You can't really be in charge – that's like slavery!' The difference was discussed. Another example was when a mainstream teacher wrote a note in the student's book: 'See me at the end of the lesson.' The student 'saw' the teacher and left the class, following the teacher's instructions exactly. The teacher was not specific; 'Come and speak with me at the end of the lesson and we can talk about this piece of work' would have ensured that the message was received! Everyday spoken language is fraught with difficulty, as we neurotypical communicators use idiom, sarcasm and masses of non-verbal communication, and we have learned much of it through osmosis without being taught.

There are countless anecdotes about children with autism getting it wrong with their understanding of language. A very new teacher in the field sees a pupil kick his welly over the big fence. The sarcastic teacher says, 'Oh, that was brilliant!' and immediately the other boot goes flying over the fence. Who got it wrong? There was a student in a mainstream secondary school who was their first student with a diagnosis of autism. One of his teachers asked why he was so rude. She went on to say, 'He never listens, he is always looking at the walls or ceiling when I am talking.' It was explained that an alternative reason could have been that the student was concentrating on the words rather than on her facial expressions, hand movements or gestures. The student didn't know that the teacher needed to have a cue that he was listening; he didn't understand the unwritten rule that we look at the speaker when we are being spoken to. This is a fundamental aspect of communication that is often taken for granted. Support was provided through a simple Social Story™ (see Glossary) and the situation improved.

Confusing idioms

We use idioms frequently without even being conscious of it, let alone stopping to consider what the phrases may mean to someone who has very literal understanding, e.g. 'Butterflies in my tummy' – how does this relate to excitement? Why does the 'bees' knees' mean something really good? Do we really mean 'you can say that again'? Why would we be 'crossing that bridge when we come to it'? Trying to process this and understand what these idioms actually mean is not easy, and even worse when you are under pressure from a teacher to respond! One illustration is a boy who overheard his mother say that she laughed so hard that she thought she'd die. The next morning when she awoke, her son was sitting by the bed staring at her, and when she asked why, he said that he was checking to see whether she'd died yet! There is also the common error of responding to the question, 'Hello, is your mum there?' on receiving a telephone call, to which the reply is 'yes' and the phone is hung up. It is the right answer!

An irate parent came to school one day demanding to see the headteacher. Her son had returned from school the previous day and asked her what 'beating around the bush' meant. His teacher had used it in the classroom and he was confused but lacked the confidence to ask for an explanation. In his mother's opinion, no idioms should be used because her son had autism and took things

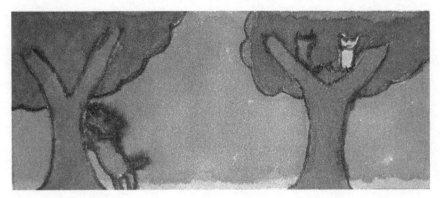

Figure 1.4 *Barking up the wrong tree – BUT what does it mean?*

literally. She explained that they never used idioms, jokes or sarcasm in their home because it was unfair to him. The head attempted to persuade her that by using these and *explaining* their meaning to her son, they would be enriching his understanding of language and preparing the way for him into adolescence and his future. Sadly, they had to agree to disagree. Using idioms can be such fun, and seeing the 'lights' come on as meaning is unfolded is exciting. There are easily accessible books and online resources to explain and illustrate idioms.

Inference

Inference is another area where difficulties in understanding can arise. When Tom was asked to take some new books into the common room, he was happy to oblige but after several minutes he had not returned. Atif was asked to go to the common room to tell Tom to return to the classroom, and he was also told that he should come back. You see, Tom had been given an instruction that did not explain that he was to take the books *and* return. We often fail to be specific and then hold the child responsible for not understanding. We ask questions like, 'Do you know where the recycling bin is?' while holding out a stack of scrap paper. The reply is a confident 'yes' and that is the end of it. We expected the paper to be taken to the bin but did we make that clear? Who is getting it wrong?

Humour

Callum loved a kind of slapstick humour – *You've Been Framed* or *Candid Camera* – and he used to roar with laughter when people tripped over. However, he hadn't really developed an understanding of many of the situations and would tell us out loud what he had done or was going to do. He gave many signals that trouble was afoot. One of his classmates had disappeared and staff were looking frantically around the school, but there was no sign of him. We got a clue when Callum was quietly saying, 'It's dark where Mickey is, it's dark' – Callum had locked Mickey in a cupboard! If Callum had been directly asked whether he knew where Mickey was he may have given the answer, but even though he knew that others were frantically looking for Mickey, he wouldn't have thought to solve the problem. Similarly, the minibus left the museum and was halfway back to school when staff realised that one young man was not on board. Panic set in with the question, 'Didn't anyone notice that Robert wasn't here?' when Keith said, 'I did, but nobody asked.'

Generally, neurotypicals are polite and try not to order others around or be insulting. It is sometimes necessary to be politely blunt – to speak the truth in a courteous way. Our language can lead to confusion. Ali was in a Year 9 class, coping well academically in a mainstream secondary school. When his maths teacher addressed the class saying, 'Would you like to take out your books?', he replied, 'No.' This was interpreted by the teacher and classmates as being cheeky and he was reprimanded. But actually, he merely answered the question. He did not want to take out his books. If the teacher had said, 'Please take out your books', Ali would have complied. Who got it wrong? Similarly, Laura was asked after snack time in a primary school, 'Laura, would you like to throw the banana peel in the bin?' You guessed it, she said, 'No' and walked away, only to be brought back and told to pick up the peel and put it in the bin. If the instruction 'Laura, peel in the bin, please' had been given, she would have responded appropriately. Who got it wrong?

Expressive and receptive language

At the beginning of the chapter, the terms *expressive* and *receptive* language were defined. This is such an important area of understanding that we'll revisit it here, emphasising the need to recognise the place of each. In autism, receptive language will often significantly lag behind a child's expressive language. This may be related to a lack of social reciprocity that many parents comment on. Social reciprocity refers to how the behaviour of one person influences and is influenced by another person and vice versa. A person with autism will often appear to tune out of conversations or social interactions and will tend to ignore voices around them, although they will perhaps be very aware of the power tool in the distance or the dog barking in a neighbour's garden. A student with autism may not pick up on the fact that the teacher is addressing the *whole* class and may miss significant pieces of information in a social context such as the classroom.

When the teacher says 'everyone', the student may not realise that that means them because *everyone* is not their name!

In order to develop receptive understanding, a typical child will develop shared attention and key preverbal skills such as reading facial expressions, imitation (or attempts at imitation), eye contact or the symbolic use of gesture (pointing). Parents label and repeat to allow their child to develop understanding. Without social reciprocity, receptive understanding will be severely impaired. If a child has difficulties with receptive language, they will experience difficulties with attention and listening, especially in a group situation. The child will find it challenging to follow instructions unless they are expressly targeted at the child. They may not respond to questions, may simply repeat the question or may have an unexpected response. In the case of one child, his answer to 99 per cent of questions asked was, 'Mmm, let me see.' He had developed this response at a very early age, and in Reception class it was cute – not so much in Year 6 or 7. It gave him time to think of the answer that he thought the adult wanted; however, all too frequently he had not been paying attention to the teacher so his answer was incorrect. He was not paying attention because he had absolutely no interest in much of what the teacher was talking about. It is frequently the case that children with autism do not follow the social norm of 'pretending' that we are interested in, for example, the Tudors and Stuarts or glaciers or the 'romantic poets'... a weakness or a strength?!

The tutor who worked with Neil would often be told, 'I am sorry, I don't know the answer because I wasn't listening because I was bored.' Neil would also say that he was listening to the birds or the grass cutter or anything that wasn't a voice. This wouldn't have gone down terribly well in a mainstream class! Neil was assisted in his attention by specifically being told that he must listen now, being given sheets and scripts that he could follow throughout the lesson and by breaking down sessions or lessons into much more 'manageable' chunks.

Tip

It is imperative that we take the time to understand each individual and modify our own communication, recognising that we, as neurotypicals, do not always have it right. As stated in the introduction to this book, Temple Grandin asks that we meet halfway – a worthy goal.

Ending on a positive and uplifting note, a four-year-old child, Meena, joined an autism-specific school with extremely limited verbal communication and social understanding. Through consistent use of interventions, high expectations and appropriate praise, through close school–home links, and through creative activities, a finely tuned curriculum and celebrations of each small step, Meena stood in her final assembly before moving to a mainstream secondary school and read a tribute to all those who had made her progress possible. She deserved the credit – she responded, learned from mistakes, tested the waters and blossomed!

Communication takeaways

- Recognise that each individual on the autism spectrum communicates in a unique way and requires bespoke understanding and support.
- Take every opportunity to step back and observe the child, their movements, their world and especially any attempts to come into our world.
- Grasp every opportunity to interact, whether being a tool to get an object or meeting a request – this gives you a way into their world.
- Learn the language; every behaviour has a communication attempt behind it and every vocalisation babble or utterance has a meaning if you can begin to understand the subtle differences in 'babbles' – these can be a building block to communication.
- Think very carefully about **your** speech – volume, tone, body language and the gestures that you use. Do you actually need them? What information do they carry? Is it positive, negative, obvious?
- The spoken language that you use must be clear and unambiguous, always explaining idioms, similes or other figures of speech that may cause confusion.
- Specifically address the person that you are speaking to by name.
- Give time to process, understand and respond.
- Recognise the importance of visual supports and use them well.

2 Socialisation: So much more than friendships

At the very heart of being human is our socialisation. We are, by nature, animals that live most successfully in 'packs', troops or families. Our success as a species is predicated on the ability to communicate and to socialise in groups. If you have a brain that processes somewhat differently from your 'pack', then there's every likelihood that you will struggle to be seen as a 'pack' member.

As discussed in the previous chapter, just making sense of words can be a challenge; the difficulty with language permeates across the spectrum in many different ways. There is the whole hidden social language that underpins so much of our socialisation, our social interactions and our social relationships. Relating to others and engaging socially is often a cause for anxiety, and the attempts to fit in with the group may result in rejection if skills are not purposefully addressed. Looking at coping strategies and facilitation of skills through practical examples will throw light on the issues involved.

Individuals on the autism spectrum vary enormously from each other but share the common difficulties in social skills of one kind or another. This impacts on:

- social interactions
- the understanding and use of non-verbal communication
- the ability to develop and maintain relationships.

Social expectations

In general, society has clearly identified – often unwritten – expectations of social conventions. Most of us learned many of these skills through osmosis: we picked things up from the stern glances and subtle messages given by family and friends. When we got it wrong, we were often reprimanded and instructed on how to get it right the next time, often learning through observation.

Sometimes the question of physical affection arises and at times it is assumed that individuals with autism do not show or want to receive affection. Once again, each person on the spectrum is an individual. One mother found it very difficult that her son, Stephan, did not accept hugs and pushed her away when she approached him for cuddles. He joined in a residential holiday, the first time being away from home and an anxious time for his family. He coped so well and, a few days after he returned home, his mother rang the school to say that he was sitting on her lap and hugging her, so much in fact that she wasn't able to accomplish anything when he was at home! We can assume that he missed his family and found a way to demonstrate it. For some, physical contact is related to the sensory aspects of touch, for others it may be related to anxiety or fear while others seek the physical contact that provides security. Respecting the individual and building a relationship of trust that may open new opportunities for affection is to be encouraged.

Friendship

The development of friendships at school is frequently an aspect that stays with us throughout our lives; however, what if the process didn't come naturally? How do you actually make a friend? It is natural for all parents to have anxieties about their children when they start school. They wonder whether they will have friends, be lonely or be invited to parties. Ordinarily, these fears lessen as children settle in and adjust to the new routine, but for the parent of a child with autism, with a disorder that makes the whole social pragmatic curriculum completely alien, the concern often continues and can be met with hurt and frustration. A number of years ago in a documentary about autism, one child expressed his loneliness by saying, 'I wish there was a shop called "Friends R Us".' It was a moving statement and should challenge all of us to do our best to facilitate positive social opportunities.

In response to the needs of a neighbour, an after-school group was organised for a four-year-old boy, Lal, who had autism, and two neurotypical peers of the same age. The session was presented visually and with consistent routine, and a true bond formed between the three children. It wasn't long before Lal showed special interest in Louise and, in anticipation of her arrival, would repeat her name as he watched through the window. Hugs were gently given. From the early days of no verbal communication, it was a moment of joy when, in the midst of a sensory activity, Lal looked at his peers and said, 'We're all having fun, aren't we?'

Sally's parents were very excited when their wee girl was going up to Reception; after a challenging year at nursery, they were sure that things would get better. Sally was just a bit different. Sally didn't join in games, she didn't share in imaginative play, she hadn't met the social goals yet, but she was just shy – she would catch up, right? But Sally had autism. How do you sit down and teach a wee girl how to initiate a conversation? How do you teach about social space? How do you teach the myriad of skills and knowledge needed to develop and maintain relationships? As mentioned previously, we don't specifically teach many of these skills to children; they pick them up, they learn from watching and observing and, perhaps most importantly, typically developing children learn from their mistakes or have the flexibility of thought that allows them to alter their behaviours.

It took Sally a very long time to learn many of the hidden aspects of friendships. It didn't come easily and there were many tears along the road, but her parents' joy at recounting how she was catching a train with her friends into the big city to buy clothes for university was both memorable and moving. This progress would not have been possible without the patient social nurturing of an understanding family and mentors, modelling socialisation and *teaching* the subtle skills that are missed.

Many aspects of developing and maintaining relationships are very similar to the difficulties that people with autism encounter with communication:

- What to say, when to say it and how to say it.
- How do you gauge the level of interest? Is it the correct topic?
- What about all the personal space and the facial expressions and body language?

We neurotypicals get it wrong frequently and we often get anxious in new social situations. We can, however, use previous experiences to quickly change and alter our social pragmatic behaviours. As we heard in the last chapter, our students will make social 'gaffes', where the social inhibitor is not always fully engaged and the social niceties are not always adhered to. How liberating would it be if we all said what we mean and didn't always beat around the bush? (Or not – there's that idiom again!)

From nursery through to college, children and young people are placed in socio-educational settings, i.e. learning in a social environment (as opposed to home schooling or online learning platforms, for example). While being on the autism spectrum does not imply a cognitive impairment, there may be significant difficulty in learning as a result of autism. Children on the spectrum frequently have difficulty with the 'hidden' curriculum and unwritten rules of socialisation. For example:

- Charlie is animatedly talking with a peer. Charlie continues to talk, standing very close to his 'friend', who keeps looking at his watch and backing away.

- Anders went to the cinema alone, unsupported, and although the cinema was virtually empty, he chose to sit immediately next to a couple.

- Sarah's mother was going out on a 'date' and asked Sarah for an opinion on her dress. Sarah told her that the dress was too tight and made her look fat!

- Anthony is sitting with some classmates at lunch in his mainstream school. He hears a peer say, 'Me and my brother went to the football last night.' Anthony tells him that it is grammatically incorrect to say 'Me and my brother'.

In the scenarios above, none of the children did anything deliberately wrong or broke any written rules – but they did make social errors that could impact on the way in which they are viewed and on their ability to be accepted and socially interact effectively with others. Without explicit instruction, these children may not realise their mistakes. There is so much that we communicate beyond the words that we say, and so many unwritten rules that we follow and expect others to follow – yet these are rarely taught.

It is important that our expectations of social events, activities and friendships are not imposed on others. Neurotypicals vary widely in their enjoyment of others, some being gregarious and others much preferring solitary time and curling up with a good book. We allow personal preference and we give others the space that they need. But what if you long for a friend and just don't quite know how to make this happen? How do we define 'friend'? Is it someone that we talk to, spend time with, share interests with or relate to on multiple levels? Part of developing social skills is creating this understanding and facilitating opportunities but *not* imposing our own personality on others.

As mentioned in Chapter 1, it is not unusual for children with autism to prefer adults to peers of their own age for engagement in conversation and activities. This is often due to the unpredictability of children, the sense of competition that they may exhibit and their reluctance to accept a peer who doesn't quite fit in. Consider breaktimes in schools, where children and young people relish the opportunity to chat and share news, discuss the latest television, fad or their favourite music and make plans for the weekend. If you don't fit into this buzz of conversation, you easily gravitate towards the perimeter of the space or towards a trusted member of staff who gives you the safety and calm that you need.

Paul attended the nursery attached to the local primary school. He could read and 'enjoyed' reading the *Daily Telegraph*. Paul could perhaps be called precocious in his knowledge of astronomy. He was still in nappies, had to be fed by his mum (only his mum at this stage) and had never interacted with children of his own age. The nursery was a completely alien environment for Paul, with no one sharing his interest in the stars and planets, so the 'home corner' was made into a 'spaceship'. Paul showed absolutely no interest or inclination to get involved with other imaginative play. He made no attempts to interact with the other children, and their attempts to engage with him were rebuffed. The sand and water and other sensory play held no interest – in fact, there was very little in the nursery that Paul showed any interest in. He would spend the couple of hours that he was attending attempting to speak with adults or walking the perimeter of the outside space. Cognitively, Paul was very able and he scored highly in educational psychology tests, but he was really struggling to access the learning as it was in a very social context. Paul struggled in mainstream schools over the next ten years. He did, however, achieve external qualifications, including A levels, through a variety of educational settings. He did get a good degree and now has a senior research position for the Met Office. Peers and their social relationships were not important to Paul but this did not prevent him from future success, and within his working environment, focus on research will not put a heavy emphasis on the social expectations of office politics.

Unstructured time

Yahir was, perhaps, at the other end of a spectrum. Where Paul had little or no interest in his 'dull' neurotypical schoolmates, Yahir was desperate to have friends, to be accepted and to join in. However, he continually found significant difficulty in friendships; the unwritten rules around interactions were alien to him. In the class situation he would frequently find himself in 'trouble' through his rather clumsy interactions – he would give his 'friends' pencils and pens and stop those who weren't 'friends' from getting them; he would shout out answers; he would hide key pieces of others' work. Yahir found that breaktimes were particularly challenging. Interactions with his classmates and others were governed by unwritten rules. Playing football, tag and other games is really difficult to navigate – how can you score goals against your 'friends'? How can you tag your friend? The rules changed at each breaktime and frequently during the break. Yahir, in his desire to have friends, was extremely vulnerable. Phrases like 'Don't tag me and I will be your friend' and 'Pass me the ball and I will be your friend' created instant dilemmas for Yahir. He would lose his temper when it went wrong (in *his* opinion) or he would become very upset that his 'friends' were 'mean' to him. A supportive teaching assistant spent a great deal of time writing the rules of tag and playground football – which was very different from PE football or Premier League football! Alternatives were found for Yahir at some breaktimes; he found that he enjoyed singular activities such as skipping – much more black and white! Eventually, Yahir began to have more successful breaks.

The unstructured times in a school are extremely challenging for children with autism, but they can be made more successful with playground buddies, clearly written guidance about how to play and the provision of activity baskets, which can result in more pleasant experiences. Breaks are training grounds for the future and vitally important in developing social interaction skills.

Tip

Working with pupils who have social interaction difficulties associated with autism requires specific and targeted work if the skills and knowledge necessary to translate into everyday socialisation are to be developed. The onus of this will be on staff, but drawing in peers to be part of modelling and support is a valuable resource that is too often overlooked.

Social interaction

There are many young people with autism who have unusual, idiosyncratic or individual responses to verbal communication. This development of language can be a double-edged sword. Brian was in many top streams and was seen as a high achiever. He was, however, beginning to encounter some very serious challenges with social interaction – he was being bullied quite badly and was reacting physically to the 'bullies'. Brian was of Chinese ancestry, his parents had very limited English and Brian was seen as the family's translator.

He spoke absolutely perfect BBC English, very similar to the stereotypical 1930s radio announcers. This made him stand out somewhat in a secondary school in north-west England. Brian had received a diagnosis of Asperger syndrome in his primary school and had largely been very well supported by his peers, his teachers and the wider school community. Unfortunately, adolescence had put significant additional challenges on Brian and he struggled to maintain his placement at the school. As an example of the social interaction difficulties and getting the 'wrong end of the stick', Brian was observing breaktime from the security of the library (his favourite place in school) and got extremely agitated when he saw a teacher 'steal' crisps from a pupil. Brian wanted to go straight to the headteacher and the police. His interpretation was that the PE teacher had just walked past and taken crisps from an opened bag in a student's hands – and this was theft, bullying and outrageous! An alternative view could be that the PE teacher was sharing the crisps and having a joke – a scenario supported by other aspects of the situation overlooked by Brian, such as the teacher and students laughing, the body language and other non-verbal communication going on throughout the episode. The scenario highlights the difficulties in interpreting communication and recognising that it is not merely the spoken word involved in social communication. Brian needed support to understand the reality of what happened – an opportunity to debrief, recognise the hidden messages that he missed and explore other scenarios that would help him in the future.

Margaret's introduction to school was in a mainstream nursery class that incorporated a specialist ASD base. Many of her interactions with her peers were negative: taking away others' toys, walking through the middle of groups in pursuit of something of interest, unintentionally breaking craft projects or models, etc. Gradually, being supported to recognise the emotions of the other children and being encouraged to apologise, she was more included and accepted. The playground was, at first, overwhelming. Margaret would watch from afar or grab something of interest like a hoop or ball that was being used by others. She began to gravitate away from her same-age peers to the older girls, Years 5 and 6, and they adored her. One day she took the hand of one, joined it to another and then another and another. In her basic language, she said, 'Stay there.' She went to the front of the line of girls, turned back to them and said, 'Choo choo', pulling them through the playground as a well-formed train. She loved it! They loved it! And it became a regular feature of play, with the girls gradually introducing new activities to Margaret.

Peer support

What a gift it is when an understanding peer or group of peers befriends the pupil with autism and helps to bridge the gap with a wider circle of peers. Unfortunately, this is not the common pattern, but it is possible to facilitate peer support in a number of ways. A pupil in a mainstream primary school befriended Eric, a peer on the autism spectrum, and became a valued support. For example, he always sat next to Eric in assembly and when Eric interrupted the headteacher, he would show him an A5-size laminated QUIET symbol and smile at him – and it worked every time! No reprimand, no big fuss, just a simple, friendly reminder. Visuals can, as discussed in Chapter 1, be extremely useful.

Helping to create a supportive environment and to enable the ethos that engenders respect between children and young people within schools, communities, families and friendships is essential to acceptance and inclusion. It paves the way for developing relationships and ensuring that social opportunities are both provided and nurtured. Observing social skills being generalised and witnessing collaborative learning between students demonstrates progress, as in a pupil who said to his food technology partner, 'How about I wash and you dry?', referring to the dishes and cooking equipment that needed clearing away. Shared responsibility, negotiation and working together may not come easily but they can be developed. Similarly, at playtime, a child pinched a hat from the head of another child and teased him with it. A peer who noticed the situation came along and said, 'Think about it. That must make her feel very sad. You should say you are sorry,' and the incident was resolved.

The trouble with teams

One of the common challenges that arises for individuals with autism is the struggle with participating in team sports and group activities. Does everyone have to be part of a team? Are solo activities acceptable? Once again, neurotypicals seem to be able to choose freely while we often feel that we have to impose these things on individuals with autism. On the other hand, helping to facilitate group involvement can have positive outcomes and open up new experiences that are enjoyed. Being sensitive to when, what and how is important.

The fear of losing and the reliance on unpredictable others have prevented many people with autism from participating in team sports or pastimes. Wayne came from a family of ardent sports fans: football in the winter and cricket in the summer. The family had season tickets for a top Premier League side and were in regular attendance at county or test matches. Wayne didn't really get the whole football or cricket aspect but he absolutely loved going – his statistical knowledge of the teams, players and scores was awesome. He got a great deal from the social side of following his team across the country and he was a vital member of the pub quiz team!

On the individual side of the argument, football or netball may be very difficult to participate in. The give and take of being flexible and always being aware of teammates can be a challenge too far. But we do want to promote physical fitness. One group of young people who declined team participation found exercise equipment, recording statistics and meeting personal goals to be exhilarating. This can lead to ongoing personal fitness in the years ahead, giving a sense of success and potentially meeting with others who share the interest. Swimming, cycling and walking can also lead to 'comfortable' activities and sharing with like-minded people.

Many and varied experiences are created for schoolchildren and help to nurture the skills of team-building and cooperation, both of these encouraging social understanding. The Forest School programmes that have been developed give regular opportunities for children to develop self-confidence and self-esteem while working alongside others, problem-solving and sharing resources. Being part of a group, selected carefully to ensure that peers are encouraging and supportive, can help a child to blossom. In one playground, a group were thoroughly enjoying a parachute activity that was fully inclusive, with one child wearing a forehead camera to record the event for the children to revisit the fun that they were having. Making group activities enticing and memorable has outcomes in the positive acceptance of being part of a team.

Vulnerability

Sadly, there are many examples that show people with autism as vulnerable to exploitation, isolation or victimisation. Bullying in schools is often reported and a lack of understanding can result in issues in the community, including a lack of welcome in social and organised activities. Individuals with autism can be more at risk of bullying because they will tend to communicate and interact with their peers differently; typically these differences will become more noticeable as the children move through school. A difficulty in reading facial expressions and misunderstanding non-verbal communication, the frequency of solitary play and, sometimes, unusual body movements or noises (sometimes referred to as 'stimming') add to the rejection that is faced. Take, for example, Len, who came to school one Monday with a black eye. He explained that he had been riding his bicycle near his home, alone. A group of other teens were chatting on the corner and when he noticed them he yelled, 'Who do you think you're looking at?' in an aggressive manner. They retaliated with a scuffle. We reviewed the situation together and discussed what else he could have done when he saw them. A peer suggested that he could have just said 'hello' and he did recognise that maybe he got it wrong. The sad thing is that Len became reluctant to ride his bicycle in fear of seeing them again.

Lucas enjoyed walking locally but on one occasion he wandered a bit further from home and was pacing on an unknown street. It happened that one of the residents recognised him from seeing him with his mother in local shops. She asked whether he wanted some help but he told her, rightly, that he was not allowed to talk to strangers. She then suggested that he could come in for a drink and a biscuit and they could ring his mum. All of a sudden, the rule about strangers was forgotten and in he went. Lucas was safe, but he may not have been. When his mother relayed this incident to his school, she asked for the school's support to emphasise stranger danger and this was addressed with a group of his peers.

Tip

Helping Lucas and others to *generalise* the rules is essential to help protect individuals from danger and from being taken advantage of.

The ability to generalise or transfer information and facts from one context to another is an important aspect of developing independence and navigating daily experiences. In the above situation, helping Lucas and others to *generalise* the rules is essential to help protect individuals from danger and from being taken advantage of.

Charles, like Yahir discussed previously, wanted to have friends and wanted to be able to go out like his peers. He had very clear expectations of what a 14-year-old boy was supposed to be up to. The trouble was that his expectations came from television, and were not necessarily the good, wholesome role models needed. Charles's 'friends' were involved in petty vandalism, smoking and most aspects of 'antisocial behaviour' found in deprived inner cities. The relationship between Charles and his mother was becoming increasingly difficult. His behaviour at school was deteriorating and becoming much more challenging. Charles was not making good choices. Increasingly, outside agencies were getting involved and, eventually, the police and social services took control and he was placed into the care of the local authority. Charles had wanted friends and was not able to discriminate between who was a good, safe friend and those who were exploiting him. He would do 'anything' to have friends, to do the things that 14-year-olds are meant to do; unfortunately, they were the wrong things.

Some parents have expressed that a positive aspect of their teenage children with autism is that they are not preoccupied with the latest fashion and hairstyles. This can reduce the peer pressure often found in teens. The other side of that is that it may cause the young person to stand out and provide an opportunity for less kind peers to ridicule. If only we were able to teach the skills of acceptance, tolerance, kindness and inclusion to neurotypical peers. Increasing understanding and far greater acceptance of autism in schools and wider society are key in reducing bullying, exclusions and social isolation.

James was admitted to an autism specialist school from a mainstream secondary, where he had been the victim of bullying on a number of occasions. He was a capable young man with artistic ability beyond his years, but his tone of voice was without inflection and his answer to almost any question was a very flat, 'It were alright.' He stood out. It took a long time for James to regain confidence, to feel accepted and to build up trust with his peer group. When you are not fully accepted, are victimised or retreat into yourself, it is very difficult to develop social competence. In his new environment, James went from strength to strength, became relaxed and regained trust in those around him.

Turn-taking

Similar to the frustration of participating in teams, turn-taking is another area that can be a stumbling block for children with autism. Winning and losing can be fraught with anxiety – especially losing! We often think of learning targets as being related to the academic curriculum, when, in fact, social communication targets such as 'winning and losing' are essential. The emphasis means that teaching such skills and developing coping strategies is taken seriously. Zahra was paired with a peer to develop the skills of turn-taking. When she won a game she was elated and exuberantly shouted, 'I won! I won!', much to the annoyance of her partner. When she lost it was not unusual for the game to be thrown to the floor and tears to be shed. Working with her to understand sportsmanship took time but was eventually successful. She reached a place where she accepted losing by complementing the winner with 'Well played' and toned down her joy at winning. If she had just been reprimanded for her previous actions or denied the opportunity to engage with her peers, these lessons would not have been learned.

Visual supports can be so helpful for turn-taking. Within one observed group, each child had a turn-taking visual to remind them of the rules of the activity. Each member of the group was continuously engaged, cooperative and motivated through the activity itself and the appropriate praise was offered. In another, a turn-taking visual using pupil photographs was used to support the session, while in another an object was passed – a tactile ball – to the person who had the next turn. This not only designated the individual but also offered a sense of comfort.

Tip

Such easily made tools to support the target through concrete and visual means should not be overlooked. They enable success and create positive opportunities rather than frustration.

The playground offers great opportunities to help with waiting and turn-taking. In one setting, for example, the cycles were very popular and when an outside choice board was developed with photographs of the equipment available, children brought their choice to a member of staff and, if necessary, it was exchanged for a wait symbol while the child on the cycle was given a two-minute warning to finish. It may seem hard to believe, but the system worked so well with the wait and exchange that it enabled turn-taking to work smoothly. Staff regularly encouraged children to socialise through engaging together to use 'interactive' equipment, such as a seesaw or shared swing.

Learning to participate with others may not come naturally but it can be facilitated in many ways. While it is important to individualise activities and projects, there are also times when children and young people should be encouraged to share what they are working on and share resources and, through this, make social links with others. It is not uncommon for a child or young person with autism to have one-to-one support from a teaching assistant. This is something to celebrate but a word of caution is essential. If this support results in the child being isolated from peers or not included in paired and group activities, it can be detrimental to progress in socialisation.

These skills cannot be learned in isolation, and dependency on an adult removes both independence and the opportunity to develop problem-solving skills – essential building blocks for future life skills. Encouraging rather than limiting engagement with peers and sharing equipment, space and interests contributes to social development.

Special interests

As discussed on page 18, many individuals with autism develop an area of special interest that dominates thought and action. In some cases, this is long term while with others, it can change regularly or periodically. These topics can be a way to support social connections rather than prohibit them. Manoeuvring situations to create an opportunity to share the interest and work on a mutual project can be bonding and affirming. For example, an interest in LEGO® can lead to working together to build models, share the bricks and negotiate pieces. The development of LEGO® therapy has helped many groups to be engaged with accepting different roles and communicating instructions. In one observed session, the resources were very well organised and group members had the opportunity to play each of the roles – builder, buyer and director. They were encouraged to listen, look and help each other by repeating an instruction if needed. Laminated A4 visuals supported for colour, size and position (on, next to, etc.). Each task was stored in a zip wallet to ensure that the appropriate materials were available. The task was successful and, more importantly, fully enjoyed with staff oversight, but the students took responsibility to complete the task.

Perspective

One of the basic difficulties with engaging with others is recognising the perspective of others and giving it value. Yahir had a bespoke piece of work on developing his ability to see others' perspectives and viewpoints. An ability to 'read others' minds' is vital in translating the social world. Gradually, Yahir developed his 'theory of mind' ability to understand what another person is thinking and that others have different perspectives, and misunderstandings became less frequent. It requires sensitive and skilful staff to help autistic children to find a way through the difficulties in understanding how others may be feeling and to understand that their beliefs, interests and experiences may be different from their own. This 'theory of mind' is where a lot of children can face conflict and where inappropriate responses begin. Many autistic children struggle with others coming to different conclusions or 'agreeing to disagree'. It may not be possible to teach the child to actually understand another person's point of view – the main goal is to help them to recognise that it may just be different and accept that.

Rigid rules

Generally, neurotypicals both accept and break rules. We are flexible in the way in which we interpret things and can agree, for example, to alter the rules of a game. This is not always the case for individuals with autism and can be very frustrating for them to cope with.

Tony was 'coping' with mainstream school, particularly enjoying physics, maths and chemistry, but he was really struggling with other students not following the school rules. He found it difficult not to intervene with students and teachers if they made a minor infraction. Because of this, he could be seen as pedantic – he may pick up on anything from the grammatical errors of others to a pupil walking on the wrong side of the corridor. Some of these infractions did actually go against the supposed order of things but some caused him difficulty due to his perception of a situation. He became more and more isolated and it was suggested that Tony wrote the 'mistakes' down in a small book and they were then discussed with a teacher (a very good maths teacher who may have had some similar difficulties…). The 'crimes' were categorised into 'What I can control' and 'What I cannot control'. This simple intervention made a huge difference to Tony's time at secondary school (a little footnote – he became a prefect and relished his job on the corridor patrol!). Tony is likely to continue to struggle with the inflexibility of his thinking around what rules and social norms are, but if time is taken to explain and exercise patience, he will be given the opportunity to progress further.

For both peers and those supporting individuals on the autism spectrum, there are times when exasperation sets in because the person demands control and wants others to fall into line. One teenage student would emphatically state, 'If you would just do what I say, everything would be fine around here.' The teacher remained calm and chose her words carefully and offered a time to chat about his concerns. For others in the group, the demands of only one way to think and do inevitably caused friction. These issues also arise in family settings, such as Zane's home. There were four televisions in the house – kitchen, lounge, parents' bedroom and Zane's bedroom. When he chose to watch a favourite programme, he went from room to room insisting that every television was on the same channel – *his* channel. He would listen carefully from the door of his room and if one of his parents switched over, he immediately went to reprimand them and turn it back. In a situation like this, a Social Story™, explaining that Zane can choose the programme that he wants to watch in his bedroom, that his parents can choose what to watch in other rooms and that sometimes they may enjoy sharing a programme together, can be very helpful. Social Stories™ are expressed positively and are reviewed regularly to embed the ideas. Neglecting to find ways in which to address control issues can result in regret, as the individual desires to take over in inappropriate ways.

Greetings

Greetings were addressed in Chapter 1 but it is worth considering the topic here, since greeting others is an accepted and, to a degree, expected social convention. If the individual is aloof or fails to notice the presence of others and acknowledge them, it can set up barriers that lead to rejection. Finding ways to address this and encourage the recognition of others is very 'doable', through the use of prompts, posters, role play and humour. One colleague worked hard on this with a group of early teens and followed up the sessions by using her facial expression and exaggerated smiles to give a clue to what she was waiting for – a 'good morning' greeting. One younger pupil had his own way of saying goodbye at the end of the day: 'You'll miss me when I'm gone.' We did!

When working with young children and often throughout special education settings, 'good morning' sessions provide a platform for helping pupils to recognise self, others and emotions. Sometimes, mirrors are used for children to look at their own image, to comment on whether their reflection expresses happy or sad, further enhanced with the use of symbols depicting the emotions for matching and labelling. In other sessions, images on the whiteboard of pupils shaking hands, giving high fives and acknowledging each other are used, followed by staff and pupils participating in their choice of action.

Facial expression

Reading faces can be so confusing, and when we are trying to convey a message through facial expression it is often lost or misinterpreted. Creatively developing ways to address this area of difficulty is essential. One of the best resources we possess is our face, and by demonstrating through exaggeration and explaining 'the look' of fear, surprise, excitement, etc., naming the expression and encouraging it to be mirrored, meaning can be gleaned. Similarly, we can give meaning to the expression on the face of the child. A teacher noticed Mandy with a very sad expression on her face and asked whether she was OK. Mandy's reply was, 'How did you know I was sad?' What an amazing teaching opportunity!

One student told a member of staff that he looked cross. The teacher acknowledged that he was not smiling but that it was his thinking face – another opportunity to address facial expression. Another would, in an exaggerated way, widen her eyes when assessing students' work, to which one lad responded, 'No, not the terrible eyes!' It became a moment of humour that was shared across the group.

Observing a session in a special needs school, the group were watching an excerpt from *The Lion King* film. Simba had tears running down his face and one of the children asked the teacher why there was water coming from his eyes. The teacher explained that they were tears and began a discussion about when and why people shed tears. A great opportunity to discuss emotion and facial expression was grasped. In another session, a pupil was encouraged to take the lead and ask peers how they were feeling and why they were feeling this way. A range of visual supports of facial expressions were used to prompt matching. Staff were mindful to sit back and were happy to give pupils time to process information and correct themselves and each other if needed.

Tip

Once again, the importance of using visuals comes to the fore. Thousands of faces have been gleaned from magazines, representing all ages, all genders and all cultures, and been used to sort into facial expression, to discriminate between young and old, male and female and to become able to attach meaning to the looks of fear, pride, calm, happy, angry and so on. Another layer of learning becomes possible from this, which is to then ask why you think he looks angry, sad, excited, etc. In this way, the understanding moves beyond labelling to attaching meaning and working to support the concerns of misinterpretation that have been mentioned previously. There is a wide range of professionally produced posters and resources available to support in this area.

One issue that arises at times is the misinterpretation of kindness and smiling. That may sound odd but, if an individual on the autism spectrum receives kindness from a peer or, for example, from a waitress or receptionist, they may interpret that as affection and assume interest beyond friendliness and an opportunity for a boyfriend or girlfriend. The reality, if pursued, is then very confusing and hurtful; this is something to be watched for and addressed if recognised.

Humour

There are those who stereotype people on the autism spectrum as 'humourless'. Although there is little doubt that people with autism may understand and use humour differently from neurotypicals, this does not remove humour from their lives. Take Manni, for example. He loved the sociability of his primary school, he loved to be at the centre of things and, in particular, he loved to tell jokes. His school was really supportive and sought to develop his sociability through active involvement in both school council and school parliament. He took great joy in showing visitors and parents around the school and was largely appropriate in his joke-telling. His joke material was a wee bit old-school, and he felt it necessary to explain why the joke was hilarious if he thought that people were not laughing sufficiently. Manni is an example showing that people with autism can and do use humour to connect with other individuals and the wider community. A lively and sociable teenager called Leigh had a collection of joke books which he enjoyed reading at home. Every morning when arriving at school he would begin to share the jokes that he had read the evening before. Most were appreciated by his peers and staff and everyone had a good laugh. He loved it when someone responded with 'I don't get it', giving him the opportunity to explain.

Working one to one in a quiet area with Fiona, her teacher was called to the phone and briefly left the space where they were working. When she returned, they carried on with the task and it was only later, when finished, that the teacher struggled to leave her chair. Fiona was suppressing a giggle when the teacher discovered that Fiona had liberally spread glue on the chair when she was distracted. Fortunately, the teacher also had a good sense of humour and they laughed together. Fiona cleaned the chair while the teacher turned her skirt around to scrub it at the sink. No harm done! The teacher returned to her office to host a meeting and throughout the rest of the morning sat on a very damp skirt!

Working with a group of teens who reflected the autism spectrum in differing ways was not always easy, but they began to bond over time and had many enjoyable times at breaks in a small common room. Word association became part of the routine and often led to fits of laughter when a unique and humorous word followed another. For example, bacon was followed by 'Babe'! Most thought it was hilarious, while a couple of students needed to be introduced to why Babe and bacon were linked.

Added extras

In a school context, to see outdoor areas with younger pupils enjoying talking and playing together at break is encouraging. Carefully designed playgrounds with clearly demarcated areas, including quiet areas and sensory gardens, balanced with areas to promote physical activity and support the wellbeing of the pupils, really enhance social opportunities. For older students, providing space to chill or be active and to have conversation, facilitated by a member of staff who draws each into some level of relating, reaps benefits. Many instances of excellent social and communicative opportunities are evident in schools, such as lunch sessions where students are encouraged to discuss what they are afraid of and reassure one another, or staff facilitating discussions on current news topics and helping young people to find common ground.

The 'added extras' that many schools invest in are worth their weight in gold for enhancing social opportunities. Lunchtime clubs continue routine during a time that can be challenging if totally unstructured. One school developed a hairdressers club that offered interaction, skills and role play. The receptionist had a book to make appointments, style books were enjoyed by those waiting and the equipment was safe and sanitary. Cooking groups support life skills, offer opportunities to explore new tastes and develop cooperation. There are endless examples of opportunities to focus on social communication and shared interests.

A school hosted a youth club for young people with autism; the group offered console games, pool, table tennis and other more structured activities that could be dropped into as the youngsters pleased. Parents could take themselves off to another classroom, and have a brew and a chat. Social opportunities for parents and the opportunity to be with others who understand some of the unique issues and anxieties are a bonus, especially when they have confidence that their children are in a safe and well-supported environment. The most popular activity by far was the consoles. The youngsters communicated online although they were sitting next to each other!

Perhaps the most successful example of social development is the opportunity to take a group of children and young people on residential breaks. When such a venture is planned, it can be somewhat daunting for staff and parents alike. Will the pupils cope? Will the families cope? Will the staff cope? Of course, such an undertaking has to be meticulously planned, from the journey, to the risk assessment of the venue and activities, to sleeping arrangements, meals and staff ratio, thinking through every eventuality.

The group returned three days later absolutely exhausted and exhilarated. The students slept well, many better than at home. The group ate well, many better than at home. They enjoyed the activities and new environments. There was a sense of bonding that took place. On the return to school, nervous families and carers were relieved to welcome their charges home after waiting in the car park for stories of upset and tears – and were shocked not to receive them. Subsequent residential breaks were also positive, with many more staff volunteers than are needed. For the teenage group, the social connections and cementing of relationships following one venture were obvious and enabled a stronger sense of group cohesion and awareness of each other.

Community

The community and local area also provide a resource for developing social connections and enabling life skills that will serve students well for the future. Becoming familiar with local leisure centres, cafés, shops and outdoor spaces offers exposure to a wide range of venues to explore away from the confines of home and school. On one café visit, when a group were rehearsing the social skills of please and thank you, independence in ordering and conversing at the table, they were surprised to find that their bill had been paid by a fellow diner. He quietly approached the staff and said that he was so impressed with the young people that he wanted to reward them and thank the staff for the care that they were demonstrating. All of the group were rightly very proud.

Adolescence

New challenges are faced in adolescence, and supporting these changes, some of which can be frightening, is absolutely essential to making these life transitions. One child was so anxious about becoming a man that he was trying not to grow by putting heavy objects on his head. He needed support from Child and Adolescent Mental Health Services (CAMHS) to gain perspective on this natural phase of development. By explaining menstruation through the use of visuals and keeping it low key, there was good success with female students. A cartoon-based video, using catchy tunes and phrases to get attention, explained hygiene and was an excellent way to get the message home. One of the phrases, as armpits were lit up at a disco, was 'Some of your bits ain't nice!' While having lunch with a teenage student after attending a meeting with him, he noticed a young couple walking past and immediately laughed and commented that 'some of their bits weren't nice'. This led to a conversation on male–female relationships and he explained that he didn't think he would ever have a girlfriend because he didn't like getting too close to people – a realistic comment on himself at that age.

It is a great frustration that even after many awareness campaigns and information provided through charities, education and social care, only *16 per cent* of autistic adults are in full-time paid employment (National Autistic Society, 2016). Like children and young people, they often feel vulnerable, and many of the challenges are related to social communication. Focus, punctuality, work ethic and commitment can be outstanding but neurotypicals seem to expect the workplace to be a social ground and many people with autism fail to fit in and be accepted. One young woman in an office was puzzled and annoyed that a colleague complimented her on her new shoes – what did that have to do with work? A man in a shared office context began to send emails to his line manager whenever a colleague was taking too long at coffee break, made too many trips to the toilet or made a personal telephone call. If the rules were not followed to the letter, he could not cope, and this inflexibility created tension in the workplace.

Too often, individuals on the autism spectrum are isolated from peers – at any age. This is often unintentional but results from the person lacking the skills to break into the group – the social aspects that lead to building relationships. We need understanding, informed, sympathetic employers to step up and provide opportunities for individuals on the autism spectrum.

Practising social skills and social communication in the classroom and within the home environment (in a safe, non-judgemental way) and then taking those practised skills out into the wider community with some sensitive support is one way to bridge the gap. Social translating is giving feedback on situations that have taken place – sometimes videoed – and then discussing it. While neurotypicals have the ability to 'read minds' and use past experiences and prior knowledge to impact on social situations, people with autism often find this hugely challenging.

Social settings

Ian went to the funeral of his grandmother. He was well regulated throughout; however, the vicar inadvertently gave Ian a prompt that led to fits of giggles and laughter. Ian was simply remembering some really happy times that he had had with Grandma – the vicar had said something along the lines of 'remember the happy times...'. It is generally socially unacceptable to laugh at a funeral but Ian had never been 'taught' that social norm! Lucy embarrassed her aunt by commenting on her facial hair in public at a family event. Before the next family gathering, her parents went through the social expectations and reminded her *not* to say anything to her aunt about her facial hair, a sensitive issue. When her mother overheard her say to her uncle, sitting next to the aunt, 'Aunt Maureen still has a lot of hair on her face, doesn't she?', her mother was understandably annoyed. She took Lucy to one side to remind her of the previous conversation, and Lucy replied, 'But I didn't say anything to Aunt Maureen.' This was, of course, true; it was the literal interpretation of what her mother had said. Lucy's mum learned a valuable lesson that day. She realised that she had to be clear in how she was explaining social communication and that she had to do her best to generalise the rules.

We all get it wrong sometimes. It's hard to imagine that anyone has not made a social *faux pas* and regretted something that was said or done socially. Sometimes these anecdotes become the stories that we tell when we laugh at ourselves. But when social communication is a challenge that results in isolation, exclusion and vulnerability, we need to do everything within our power to ameliorate it. By helping the individual to reflect on the situation that went wrong, to talk it through, debrief and explain in ways that the person can understand, we are contributing to wellbeing and access to positive opportunities.

Socialisation takeaways

- Remember that social skills cannot be taught in isolation.
- Respect the individual and their interests and needs.
- Be alert to social errors – don't ignore them.
- Take time to explain and consider ways in which to reduce future repetition of errors.
- Use appropriate communication skills when addressing the issues, based on the needs of the individual.
- Allow processing time.
- Use well-chosen visuals.
- Facilitate opportunities for recognising facial expression and use your face as a resource.
- Provide as many varied social opportunities as possible.
- Encourage shared experiences and nurture relationships.
- Be flexible; the person with autism finds this very difficult, so we, as neurotypicals, need to be even more flexible.
- Autism has many strengths – **look for the ability and not the disability**.

3 Flexibility: So much more than imagination

We all find change difficult and often prefer things to stay the same, but when this inflexibility leads to high anxiety and inhibits opportunities, it can play havoc with the lives of the individual, family and friends. This chapter will consider examples that clarify these issues and show creative solutions, demonstrating that flexible ways forward can be found and encouraging the reader not to give up.

Some points to consider:

- Flexibility is the ability to accept change and recognise the perspective of others.
- Anxiety can be a result of unpredictability, the unexpected or change.
- Imagining is a challenge, as it demands moving from the concrete to the abstract.
- Special interests can be distractions or turned to positive incentives.

This book, as mentioned in the introduction, is being written during the biggest crisis that the world has known for many decades. We are in lockdown, with social distancing, staying safe and keeping others safe, celebrating front-line workers and grieving the loss of many friends and family. A price is being paid economically, socially and emotionally, and this is highly evident in the world of autism. Parents who are home-schooling are struggling to replicate the daily routine and structure of school. Families with children in residential care have had to make choices about whether to have many weeks of not visiting or disrupting routine totally by taking their family member home to care for. Very difficult decisions. Trying to support individuals with autism who find change difficult requires consistent and creative planning, great understanding and patience. Getting into the mindset of the person, seeing things from their perspective and determining to make life predictable is a gift that you can offer.

Social imagination allows us to make sense of abstract thoughts and concepts, and allows us to predict and adapt our behaviours in day-to-day living. An impairment in social imagination makes interaction, communication and flexible thinking hugely challenging. People with autism try to control their own environments but this is impossible to do in a wider context. A mind that struggles with flexibility does not easily shift and adapt to change.

Need for routine and predictability

Schools, by their very nature, are places of routine, with timetables, rules, structure and discipline. Or are they? In many respects, the answer is yes, but they also need to be places of flexibility, and for most of the students this is not a problem. Some of the daily changes include absent teachers covered by supply or cover staff, dinner menus being altered, areas of the school being out of use for exams, equipment shortages for a group and the inevitable flexibility of a teacher needing to change the focus of the lesson. For the vast majority of the students these things will be taken in their stride, but to a young person on the autism spectrum, these can be monumental and create anxiety as well as significantly interfering with their ability to learn.

Recognising that these focus and attention issues require reasonable adjustments to be made and being sensitive enough to forewarn of change and understand that there is a need to explain, often through visual means, go a long way to reduce the anxiety. This can be a bigger challenge in mainstream schools, while most special schools are geared up for routine and provide a high level of individualised and group structure. In fact, the emphasis there has to be on helping to develop flexibility! For example, some special schools for secondary-aged students follow a rigid structure that enables students to predict what is ahead and subsequently reduces anxiety. The day begins with an opportunity for students to relax and read, choose an activity in the games room or chat with peers and staff in the canteen while everyone gathers. After a short registration period, where staff explain whether and why any students are expected to be late or are absent, any changes to the school day are communicated to the students before they move to their learning sessions. Throughout the day this routine is followed and changes are explained as they occur. For example, when a member of staff had to leave before the afternoon sessions began, her group were well informed of what arrangements had been made and accepted this without incident. An adult service was making excellent use of modern smartphone technology to develop independence in their service users. An app using flow charts and organograms helped in problem-solving and managing unforeseen changes and provided a strong visual structure to daily routines, allowing a very appropriate methodology to solve the frequent problem of communicating change.

In an educational setting, these social imagination and flexibility issues can manifest themselves in difficulties with attention. Christopher, mentioned previously, was having some difficulty in his mainstream secondary. He found it hard to focus on his teachers when they were speaking, partially because of the confusion around what to focus on, with his heightened level of arousal distracting him from the teacher's words. Christopher also explained that he would lose focus watching the dust in the sunbeams or the strange patterns that he could see on the desks or just about anything other than the teacher. Clearly in a 'traditional' chalk and talk class, this could be a massive issue, with English and modern foreign languages (MFL) being particularly problematic for him. Switching focus from teacher to pupil, to text, to board to the previous week's learning was very challenging. His support assistant in English had a number of strategies to help focus: scripts, bullet points on previous learning, etc. However, there can be a danger that the support assistant reduces independence, and having an assistant glued to the child's side can be a real issue. Skilled and sensitive support assistants can be a game-changer and are worth their weight in gold! Christopher was very well supported in English – a combination of astute teacher, good support and effective interventions enabled Christopher to stay focused and to achieve. Contrast this with MFL, where his support assistant did everything for him, significantly impacting his progress.

Anxiety

Anxiety is a very significant issue around the need for predictability and routine; uncertainty causes anxiety and anxiety can manifest itself in a variety of ways. Alvin was very routine-bound and became extremely anxious if things were not exactly as he expected. For example, if his taxi did not arrive in the correct order – it had to be third in the queue at the end of the day – a major meltdown would ensue, with Alvin's mum having a very difficult evening. He could not eat his packed lunch if it was not in the 'right' place or if things inside the box had moved. As Alvin ate such a restricted diet, it was important that he did eat, and to that end considerable time was spent ensuring that everything was just right. Lots of photographs and consultation with Alvin's mum ensured that his routines were met. Alvin had huge anxiety when visiting new places, trying new experiences and attempting new foods. Preparation through photographs, and making sure that there was enough predictability within the activity for Alvin's anxieties to be reduced as much as possible, allowed a very gradual broadening of Alvin's limited horizons.

Any deviation from any of the specifics, even one almost undetectable to a neurotypical individual, can result in enormous anxiety from a child with autism. Adherence to routine becomes obsessively important and any sort of change can be a cause for alarm.

Unstructured time

Chapter 2 addressed the challenges of unstructured time and the need to facilitate socialisation and reduce the anxiety that the lack of routine causes. These heightened social expectations often result in the child with autism retreating into 'stereotypical behaviour' that may help to meet the need for order and offer security. This may be displayed through repetitive movements, repeating phrases, pacing, twirling, filtering light through fingers, etc., and seems to help self-regulation and maintain order. School breaktimes are often times when a child with autism just needs a release; it is stressful and tiring to focus on the rules in a classroom setting. One pupil in a large secondary school was being picked on because he paced around the yard and flapped – not particularly cool. However, a flexible-thinking PE teacher gave the student a basketball and the flapping was exchanged for bouncing a ball. The sessions after break were more positive, as the pupil was much better regulated. We neurotypicals who are able to think flexibly need to be even more flexible for our students! We need to search for creative solutions to support the individual and respect their need for different coping strategies.

One way of doing things…

Other forms of seeking order and sameness are often observed. Julie lined up her miniature toys in a specific order – it was always the same order and if someone rearranged them it caused distress until they were back the way they belonged. The sameness brought calm and removed chaos. Marc had hundreds of action figures arranged around his bedroom and would become very distressed if they were moved, making cleaning and dusting extremely problematic. His dad took photos and when Marc was away at his respite service, whole-scale cleaning could take place with enough time to rearrange Marc's extensive collection. Distress avoided!

Morris paused at each door frame, touched the top, the right and then the left sides, stomped on the threshold and then entered. Was he testing the safety of the entrance? Perhaps. Or was it a ritual that just felt right? We don't always know the purpose. To restrict these movements or to prohibit them removes the rights of the individual to engage in their own routine and coping mechanisms.

> ### Tip
>
> **Let's be honest, we all have some little routines, habits and fidgets that we engage in – and that sometimes annoy others!**

A pathological need for routine and sameness frequently results in significant difficulties in attempting alternative ways of doing things; Joel had learned to swim with his school at a small pool in a local secondary school, yet he could not swim at all in his local leisure pool. In these very different environments, Joel couldn't transfer his swimming ability. Arthur had learned addition through one method in one class and his next teacher had a slightly different way of doing it – Arthur could not transfer his skills and knowledge from one year through to the next, significantly inhibiting his learning and progression.

Generalising

Issues relating to flexibility also relate to generalising, to recognising the similarity between items and their purpose. A further example of this is a young man who loved Cookery Club and efficiently prepared vegetables for meals. The school chopping board was a wooden rectangle and the peeler had a metal handle. When using a different kitchen and volunteering to prepare the vegetables, he was totally confused because the cutting board was round and the peeler had a plastic handle. It had to be explained that they were similar and that they served the same purpose, and once he saw them demonstrated he took over with ease. Just think of the many times that we offer resources that are, in our minds, the same, but which are not to the student with autism who has only been introduced to a different form. Will it work the same? Do I know how to use it? This is when anxiety rises and confidence reduces. We need to recognise these issues and, like the social rules, we need to teach, explain and model to widen understanding. What is a spoon? Is it the wooden one for stirring, the metal one for eating, the slotted one for straining or the plastic one for picnics?

Figure 3.1 *Different types of spoons*

There is often a sameness that is seen to be rigid – one way to do something, one accepted product or resource, and when change occurs it can cause huge anxiety. Kerry had a very restricted diet, which included a well-known brand of chocolate sweets, but when the manufacturer changed the packaging they were rejected outright. Sharon preferred rice cereal for breakfast, and in an endeavour to economise her father bought a cheaper brand and put them into the original box. Sharon instantly recognised the difference and rejected the substitution. Bhola would only eat a well-known make of crisps and could tell whenever family or school attempted a substitution – apparently, not all ready-salted crisps are the same!

It can be difficult for parents and carers when their child outgrows a favourite piece of clothing or pair of shoes and will not accept something different. It can result in short trousers and tops and too-tight footwear. One family bought the same shoes in increasing sizes to avoid the problem. For one child, it was the sadness of outgrowing *Thomas the Tank Engine* clothing. His father had a brainwave and bought labels that depicted the popular engine, and by sewing them into new clothing or on the cuff, he was as happy as could be. Creative solutions can win the day.

We met Sally in an earlier chapter. Sally was very rigid and had extremely fixed routines, and she carried the need for sameness into her diet – what she would and would not eat. She would only eat 'white' foods: white chocolate, white bread without crusts, white vanilla ice cream and yogurt, and she would only drink milk. If she was in a good place, mash or occasionally poached chicken could be added; however, the opposite was equally true: if she was stressed, she limited her diet even further. Eating is a very emotive and challenging area, particularly for parents, and mealtimes can become exceptionally stressful. Limiting diets or only eating certain foods in certain places or on specific crockery can be a major issue for family life.

Tip

It can be extremely problematic to find solutions to eating difficulties, and additional support may need to be sought. Specialist dieticians are sometimes required to offer advice. A slow and steady approach, making small changes and enticing rather than insisting is generally the way forward. A healthy diet is part of wellbeing, a goal to be strived for.

Dealing with unanticipated change

The neurotypical world is a confusing, unpredictable and ever-changing environment, and as such is immensely challenging to people who need routine and sameness to control their anxiety. The use of timetables, calendars and lists can all help in supporting children and young people to cope with the world around them. TEACCH, an acronym for Treatment and Education of Autistic and Communication Handicapped Children, is a structured programme that provides pupils and students with a framework for structuring the whole environment, colour-coding specific areas for tasks and activities. A TEACCH-based classroom is well demarcated and provides good visual support to develop independence.

There are excellent examples of highly structured TEACCH-based classrooms in many autism-specific schools and in generic special schools. Many of the principles can be adapted to be used in mainstream settings, as set out in the table below.

Why?	Individuals with ASD often process visual information more easily than verbal. TEACCH advocates using visual support, structure and cues to enable access, independence and increased understanding.
How?	Recognising the need for *structure* to be able to thrive and develop, and to create order and security in what is often a very confusing world. This is achieved through visual timetables, physical structure of environment and structure of activities.
What?	• Visual timetables • Physical clarity • Clearly structured activities • Clarity of start, finish, expectations and what is next

Marcus was in a mainstream primary school that made many adjustments and allowances to enable Marcus to participate in much of the daily life of the school. He carried a folder around with him that had colour-coded curricular areas and specified where these activities would take place, to further reduce Marcus's anxiety; expectations of work and outcomes were also clearly outlined. Over time, the school further tweaked Marcus's folder so that it became a planner, and he took this on to secondary school with him. Marcus found that he needed less information in his folder; however, he benefited from prior warning and knowledge and he specifically needed to know *where* activities were happening, *what* teachers' expectations of him were in terms of the amount of work to complete, and what was next *when* he finished. Offering a visual structure that can answer the 'where', 'when' and 'what' questions can have a big impact on reducing anxiety in a classroom.

Tony could only work if his paper was parallel to the sides of his work table, but he shared the table with another student. He persisted in reaching across the desk to straighten his peer's work. His table-mate preferred his work to be at an angle and the intrusions led to disagreements. The way forward was found by adding a piece of red tape down the centre of the table. Tony was in charge of his side

Figure 3.2 *A very simple TEACCH-style schedule*

but was not to cross the line. It was a successful and accepted solution. There are times when the insistence of sameness is not worth a battle, while others require compromise and problem-solving.

The use of visual supports can be the most effective way of developing greater flexibility in autism. Schools and services employ a variety of symbolic representations of change or surprise.

Making effective use of these visuals, supporting a positive experience and not something to be feared, will over time allow unforeseen change to become a less challenging event – small, consistent steps will have an impact. Social Stories™ have been previously mentioned, and they can be very effective as a supportive intervention for change and surprise.

In *Thinking in Pictures* (2006), Temple Grandin explains how she thinks visually, rather than in words (like a neurotypical); this pictorial imagery allows her to be very precise, excelling in scenarios where visualisation is beneficial. The drawback to this visual thinking is, however, that abstract thinking is more problematic; this in turn makes generalisation much harder.

Figure 3.3 *Symbols representing change and surprise*

Focusing on minutia

Executive functioning impacts on a person's ability to organise thoughts, behaviours and emotions, to plan, to pay attention and to inhibit inappropriate behaviours. The impact of having difficulty with executive functioning can be seen when a person with autism struggles to cope with 'change'. This includes organising, planning and bringing tasks to conclusions, as well as attending to and recalling information and being impulsive. For example, Terry was a capable student and had a high ability in maths but often failed to achieve because of the random way in which he organised his work and resources. He often forgot the equipment that he needed and, becoming frustrated with himself, he would give up and refuse to start again. By supporting him with a visual list of what was needed, a sympathetic teacher who made apparatus available and enough working space to keep things in order, he began to make and maintain progress. Richard joined his special school very early on in his school career; he was one of the school's 'more able' pupils and spent his final years of school very successfully in a mainstream setting. He secured a place at university studying maths. He had no issues regarding his academic ability to study his chosen subject, but he had no idea how to use the reading list that he was given and struggled to prioritise the workload that arose from the various courses he had to take. He experienced a great deal of stress as a result of not being able to pace his work in relation to the range of deadlines that he had been given, significantly impacting his mental health.

Wayne, as discussed previously, was a very regular attender at both Maine Road and, latterly, the Etihad. His focus was not on the football on show but rather on the detail of the games – who scored, when, the attendance and other statistical information. He was clearly fixating on the detail and not the bigger picture. There is a real positive to this aspect of autism: the fixation on detail is very attractive to many employers in the tech industries, and many large IT companies are actively seeking potential employees who are on the spectrum.

Neurotypicals use past experiences and memories to adapt behaviours or responses, while people with ASD can find it very hard to accept and cope with changes or alterations. A useful analogy to illustrate this is that our brains are like a series of filing cabinets. The individual with autism will search through all the drawers and all the files within those drawers and, to compound the difficulty, only one of the autistic person's drawers at a time will open. A neurotypical knows which drawer contains the appropriate memory or response, and a neurotypical brain can have lots of drawers open in lots of cabinets at any one time.

People with autism have an increased ability to focus attention on certain tasks. While neurotypicals may 'waste' time on some activities that appeal to them – activities such as socialising and small talk – people with autism can concentrate for extended periods of time on specific non-socially based interests. Not only do people with autism appear to have an increased capacity for extended focus, but they also tend to have an ability to hyper-focus on areas of interest, like Wayne's knowledge of the statistics of football and cricket matches. This concentration can be so intense that an individual loses track of time, other chores or the surrounding environment.

The environment

While typical mainstream classrooms are not particularly autism-friendly environments, they can be adapted with minimal impact on the rest of the class.

Think carefully about where you are asking the pupil to sit. Positioning is the first step – away from the window and busy traffic areas that cause distraction. Displays are a vitally important part of a good learning environment. With care and thought they can be accessible to all, although considering the need to direct focus to the learning rather than to the numerous distractions will take some time and practice.

Central coherence

Central coherence is explained in the introduction. In brief, it's our ability to see the 'big picture', and when this is weak, as is often the case with individuals with autism, it results in seeing the parts rather than the whole. Saul, for example, had a passion for crisp packets. The crackling sound fascinated him and gave him great joy. The difficulty was that he only saw them, regardless of the bigger context. This resulted in him running across a road to chase one that was floating in the breeze. Fortunately, the road was clear but it may not have been. On another occasion a young child was holding a packet of crisps and eating them when Saul grabbed them from her and emptied them on the ground – this, of course, resulted in tears and an angry parent. It was important to use these situations to help Saul to understand the boundaries and see that his impulses needed to take account of the surroundings and context. Barry, a capable boy with autism, was playing in nursery, using the lawnmower to cut the grass. The SaLT (speech and language therapist) asked Barry what he was using to cut the grass and, without hesitation, Barry responded with 'the handle'. Tom noticed that the colourful mat in the classroom had been turned and the pattern no longer looked right to him. He immediately set to returning it to where he thought it should be, ignoring the furniture that was on it and almost having an accident – the only thing that he noticed was the wrong colour in the wrong place. In their interactions with the environment, or in recalling information, most neurotypical individuals will recall an overall impression or the 'gist' of something in a story, an experience or a conversation. Individuals with autism frequently tend to be more – and sometimes overly – focused on small details at the expense of understanding the actual meaning or appreciating the nature of a situation or context. It is important for us, as neurotypicals, to interpret the reason for the behaviours, actions or responses, and to give meaning to them, opening up awareness of the bigger picture.

Special interests – or obsessions

We all have specific interests that we enjoy, our hobbies and pastimes. Some neurotypicals refer to these as obsessions when referring to a person with autism. The term 'special interests' is preferable, as it does not have the negative connotations of 'obsession'. The special interests are many and varied and for some they are long-lasting, while others change periodically; whichever, these can present problems.

Alistair changed his favourite foods about once every two months. He would eat only a certain brand of meat pies and then suddenly decide that he disliked them and would turn to burgers for a period of time, and then to pasta. Never a variety, never two things at the same time. His family accepted this and provided what he chose. We could debate whether this was the right decision or whether strategies should have been put in place to create a more flexible, nourishing diet, but there are times when accepting choice is the right way forward. Jacob became very interested in all forms of stationery and used all of his pocket money on paper, files, envelopes, pencils, etc. This went on for many months and the collection was building up in his bedroom but seldom used. On arrival at school one day, he said that he was a bit bored of his collection and asked whether it was wanted for the classroom. His mum was overjoyed to agree. On another occasion, Jacob took a school topic to heart when we explored recycling and made our own paper. His mother rang to ask whether we could intervene as he was going to the newsagent's, spending all of his weekly money on newspapers and immediately taking them to the recycling bin. He had understood the value of recycling but not the process of reading the newspapers before disposing of them. By discussing the situation, Jacob realised that, although his intentions were good, he could use his money for other things and encourage his family to let him recycle the papers that they purchased.

Bilal was attending a generic special school and was placed in the school's discrete autism unit. Bilal was exceptional at drawing tigers – tigers running, tigers' heads – and all from memory. Bilal would spend all day drawing, colouring or painting tigers if he was allowed to, and often at home this was what happened. He would reluctantly attempt other drawings but these were not of the quality of his tigers. His artistic skills were far above the 'norm' and a specialist art teacher became involved. With her support, Bilal achieved a GCSE in art a full 18 months before the expected chronological age, attaining a B grade. With specialist support and guidance and a great deal of work from Bilal, his special interest was

Flexibility

channelled successfully; however, there is a very sad postscript. Unfortunately, his special interest had become an obsession that overwhelmed all aspects of his life, and Bilal had a psychotic episode that resulted in him being sectioned less than a year after his exam success.

Imagination, or lack of, is often seen as part of inflexibility. This does not mean that all individuals with autism lack imagination but it can be a stumbling block. Kevin loved drawing and would often try to complete his work early to have a few minutes to turn to his sketch pad. He replicated popular superheroes and cartoon figures beautifully but *never* drew something from his own imagination and never personalised his work. On one occasion as he sat with a member of staff, it was suggested that each draw a monster. His teacher created a one-eyed, hump-backed creature while Kevin drew one of his standard villains. He then asked, 'Where did you get that from?' It was explained that it was just thought up, using imagination. Kevin was amazed. They then drew another monster together, with suggestions for a shape, then eyes, hair, etc., while Kevin developed his first ever imaginative drawing. He was thrilled and began to find ways to combine the old with the new, thus broadening his artistic horizons. Amira made a great first impression on her teacher when she visited her new school for the first time. She made a beautiful, colourful house from LEGO® which showed dexterity and imagination. When she joined the school as a pupil, she regularly selected the LEGO® when she had choice time and it soon became evident that the colourful house was the product of each session: same bricks, same colours in exactly the same places. Like Kevin's drawing above, Amira had copied a model – the photo on the original box that her set of LEGO® had come in. Only through facilitated play with members of staff did she begin to recognise that other formations were possible.

The variety of special interests is endless, and merely echoes the huge range of interests in the human mind. The special interest can become an issue when it creates difficulties in the home or at school, if the intensity and duration become 'all consuming'. This is perhaps when it tips into the 'obsession' category. Ben knew everything about World War Two but it became problematic and a challenge, however, when he became fixated on the Waffen-SS and collecting Nazi memorabilia. He spent lots of time on the internet and less and less time with his family. It all came to a head when he was ready to go out with the family dressed as a German stormtrooper. The family had a salutary lesson; they had to be far more involved in Ben's special interest and put in place boundaries and structure that allowed Ben some access to his interest but prevented it from significantly impacting on his life.

Aversions or irrational fears?

Sometimes, inflexibility is related to aversions and it is not always possible to find the root cause of the situation. Lawrence could not abide the colour green and often closed his eyes or became distressed when outside in nature. He would not walk on grass, wear the colour, use green paint or markers, etc. One morning he arrived at school in an upset state; we were finally able to discern the problem when Lawrence wept and wept as he explained that they had a new front door at home and it was green! He did not want to enter or exit through the offending door. It was the front door of the house and the one that was generally used. Chatting with his dad, we reached a consensus that Lawrence would be able to use the back door. He accepted this and just closed his eyes until he reached the side of the house.

Craig (whom we met in Chapter 1) suddenly became exceptionally challenging at home and, in particular, when the family were trying to go out. There was no obvious reason for this change – soft toy routines were the same and the outings were communicated on the family schedule. Craig's older sister spotted the problem. His dad's car had changed colour – it was exactly the same model and everything inside the car was the same, but it was just an 'updated' shade of blue. Unfortunately, there was no way to get the original company car back and the family had a difficult couple of months.

Carlo did everything possible to avoid the colour blue, a real challenge in a classroom that had blue chairs and table tops. His teacher started him with a brown-topped table and covered the blue chair with a cloth. He accepted this. Over time the cloth was reduced in size until it became a paper hand towel on the seat, and one day he took the towel and put it in the bin. Crisis over. Carlo began to realise that blue was just another colour and never looked back. Sometimes the sure and slow tactic wins the day!

It is not uncommon to come across numerous young people who have an 'extreme' reaction to loud, sudden noises. Fire alarms, sirens or car horns can result in significant meltdowns. Fireworks, balloons popping or loud dogs barking can be the start of difficult times. These are not irrational fears. These are understandable if the child has difficulty with flexibility of thought and executive functioning and a weakness in central coherence. If a neurotypical hears a dog bark, generally we consider all options based on past experiences – the filing cabinet analogy used earlier. If you have autism, every dog bark, every siren and every alarm will be different, a relatively new and unknown experience and, as such, scary!

One pupil had a very challenging end of the day, compounded when the taxi was not in the 'right' order. As Alvin, whom we met previously, became more stressed and anxious, his level of arousal was not helped by the impatient taxi driver sounding his horn. What Alvin needed was time, reassurance and acceptance – not asking too much.

When the aversion to change and the commitment to only one way of doing something takes over, it can be helpful to 'sabotage' the situation to encourage and enable flexibility. For example, it is not uncommon for individuals to only accept one route between places. This is no doubt because that's the way in which the journey has always been done, but there are times when the driver, parent or escort has to make a stop en route or there may be a diversion. The wrong turn can cause huge anxiety. The problem is that the child does not realise that there is more than one way to travel between two points. Fear sets in: fear that the vehicle is not going to the expected destination. When at all possible, if the change of direction is known, it should be explained, a reason given and the reassurance that everything is OK and the destination will be reached. Rehearsing the change of route in advance, perhaps with a visual diagram, can be helpful.

Rules and regulations!

Rules can actually be helpful because they present things in black and white – one way in which to do things. They provide predictability and reduce uncertainty. The difficulty is that we often bend the rules, and for someone who respects rules and abides by them, *our* flexibility is not appreciated. If work is to be done in pencil and a pen is allowed, the rule is broken. If there are set places to sit at lunch and someone is allowed to move to sit near a friend, the rule is broken. Unless a reason is given and the flexibility is explained, the issues can cause great distress. Explaining, for example, that Asha was feeling upset and it helped her to sit near Jean today may be an accepted reason. The 'because I said it was OK' will never be a satisfactory explanation. Archie left post-16 provision with a very strong desire to learn to drive, and there was absolutely no reason why he couldn't. He had many lessons with an outstanding instructor and he passed his test first time. However, he doesn't drive and has said that he won't because he becomes too stressed and anxious about other people who do not follow the rules – as Archie sees it, 30 means 30 and 40 means 40! He is of course right, but we are all guilty of bending rules – or at least the neurotypicals among us are.

Transitions

Transitions are often times of distress, as change and uncertainty create a sense of insecurity. There are many such times in our lives and we often focus on the larger changes like moving house, changing schools or starting a new job. There are, however, transitions throughout every day, and when change is problematic, that can mean that stress levels are often very high. For a child or young person with autism, leaving home for school, arriving at school, negotiating the building during the day and then doing the reverse trip at the end of the day is a big ask. Routines such as bedtime and meals, respite and doctors' appointments are all transitions that can feel overwhelming and confusing. Kiri found leaving home to go to school each morning very distressing, and it was heart-breaking for his parents to watch him crying as the taxi pulled away from the house. For Kiri, a schedule in his bedroom outlining the morning routine, followed by another on the inside of the front door *showed* him what was happening and, accompanied by the soothing words of family, helped him to gradually accept the daily routine and relax into it.

> ### Tip
>
> **Transitions can be well supported through the use of visuals to clearly show what is happening and to ease anxiety by making events predictable.**

It is absolutely paramount that transitions from year to year and changing from primary to secondary school are sensitively and meticulously planned.

Opportunities to visit the new setting, to be introduced to new staff, be reassured about what will remain the same and be provided with photographs to support, all help to pave the way to a smooth acceptance of the changes. When a school moved premises over the summer break, staff began in the summer term to take the children and young people to see the new site being erected. The route to the new area became familiar. Each class staff group carefully removed a display board from the current room to use in the new room to provide a familiar anchor to the old. Each pupil left for the summer break with a photograph album of the new building, their classroom, staff members and peers. Parents and carers were asked to use it over the summer to help with familiarity and ease the transition to the new setting. New children joining the school were also provided with the visuals. The transition went smoothly and everyone settled in well, making the new year start off on a very positive note.

Tip

By taking away the chaos of unpredictability and uncertainty and breaking things down to manageable, clearly identified steps, we are supporting wellbeing and reducing anxiety.

Social Stories™ have been mentioned in previous chapters and can be very supportive for transitions. One excellent example observed was for a young pupil who was extremely anxious about transition to a new respite placement. A well-written Social Story™, sensitive preparation and careful management by school staff ensured that the placement was successful. However, some parents have reported that the big transitions can be OK (the child has no control over moving class, school, etc.) and it is the small changes that can be the biggest challenge – weekend socks on a school day equals disaster! Perhaps this is one of the reasons why a very limited wardrobe can be so much less stressful.

Flexibility takeaways

- Inflexibility of thinking can have a very significant impact on all aspects of life.
- Recognise the anxiety that this causes and develop appropriate support.
- Provide routine and build in predictability.
- Where possible, warn of unexpected change and surprise.
- Neurotypical thinkers **need** to be more flexible in their thinking and creative in facilitating coping strategies.
- Flexibility can be developed – it needs time, patience and very careful planning.
- Look for opportunities to build in sabotage to support generalisation.
- Tap into 'special interests' to affirm skills and broaden opportunities.
- Fears or aversions are not in any way irrational and, through using small steps, can be reduced.
- Recognise difficulties with organisation and provide the necessary prompts to improve.
- Offer wide-ranging opportunities to extend experiences and enable the introduction of varied activities to extend flexibility.
- Preparation for changes makes the difference.

4 Sensory impact: Another challenge to overcome

Many people with autism report significant difficulties in processing everyday sensory information. Since 2013, the DSM (*Diagnostic and Statistical Manual of Mental Disorders*) has included sensory sensitivities among the diagnostic symptoms of autism. These sensory differences impact on responses, often causing anxiety, and can have a profound effect on the person's life. This chapter will look at the *eight* senses, their impact on daily life and the compensatory strategies that can positively support the individual.

> 'Sensitivity to light, sound, touch is potentially more debilitating than those disabilities related to social interaction and communication.'
>
> (Olga Bogdashina, 2003)

Recognising the impact of sensory issues, it follows that looking at both hyper- and hyposensitivities is crucial to understanding how to support and enable wellbeing. Sensory overload often results in anxiety levels rising and, in turn, coping and learning are reduced. Identifying the needs specific to the individual is essential and may require specialist sensory integration assessment and therapy (see the further reading section on page 157 for information).

One aspect that permeates each of the senses is the environment experienced by the individual. The distraction of sight, sound, odour and touch can assault the senses, create levels of discomfort and destroy the ability to function. Taste can have a profound effect on diet and nutrition. Add to this the need for movement and the issues of balance, position in space and body awareness, and you begin to recognise the high impact and distress that can occur. Schools typically strive to make the environment stimulating with colour and displays on walls, tables and even dangling above! The assault on the senses can be absolutely painful, as will be seen through examples in this chapter.

Frequently, the distractions and overstimulation are difficult to pinpoint. In each area of the senses, it takes determination to unravel the root cause of distraction or discomfort. By being a 'fly on the wall', we can sometimes identify and address these issues, enabling the individual on the autism spectrum to have a better quality of life.

Tip

When the environment supports the understanding of and is sensitive to these issues through making reasonable adjustments, the lives of individuals with autism are enhanced and inclusion is enabled.

Some points to consider:

- A high percentage of individuals with autism report sensory processing difficulties.
- Hypersensitivity refers to acute sensitivity to sensory stimuli and overload.
- Hyposensitivity refers to reduced awareness and being under-sensitive.
- Sensory issues may have an impact on comfort and concentration and create anxiety.
- Creating an environment sympathetic to sensory needs is essential.

Visual distractions

So many distractions, so many reasons to find it difficult to concentrate, be productive and access learning... as mentioned above, the environment is fraught with sensory challenges. Jamie frequently pushed his fingers into his eyes, often when he was under stress and particularly in his classroom. Jamie eventually explained that by squeezing his eyes, the patterns and 'lights' were comforting and blotted out the unpleasant 'jaggy' patterns from the fluorescent strip lights. These lights, in many classrooms and shops or other public spaces, have a very distinct colour and frequently have a 'buzz' or hum when on, worsening as they come to the end of their cycle. To help Jamie, he worked as often as possible without the lights on. There are many examples of schools updating their lighting, removing the fluorescent strips and replacing them with LED lights that have different settings, flooding the class with light that eliminates pain or discomfort. Different frequencies of white light can promote

Figure 4.1 *The five senses*

alertness, giving a calming and relaxing hue. New-build autism-specific schools make full use of natural sunlight throughout the year, using sun tubes or other innovative solutions. Venetian blinds can be problematic, with sunlight leaking through when they are half-open or half-closed, creating distraction, irritation or even pain. Jamie's eye-pressing can be extremely dangerous and can cause irreversible damage. It is thus of paramount importance that if a child is seen to be reacting in this way, the function of the behaviour is identified and effective compensatory strategies are implemented. Li was often seen to wiggle his fingers in front of his face and stare at them for periods of time. This was especially noticed when the sun was shining through the windows. Li was filtering the light and watching the dust particles in fascination. By installing blinds in the windows, this distraction was greatly reduced. These two examples demonstrate the need to understand the *individual* needs of the person and to respond with individualised solutions.

For hypersensitivity to light the use of sunglasses can help, and the variety of lens colours allows personalisation. For hyposensitivity, compensatory strategies are more challenging. Amy found that the writing on white paper became a 'grey mess' on her page and, by providing a reading lamp on her desk in her work-station, she was able to cope. Solutions in the community were much more challenging, particularly before a selection of bulbs – halogen, LED, etc. – was available, with their range of hues and 'warmths'.

It isn't just the light, the displays, the colours and the overstimulation of clutter and clashing patterns that distracts. The human face, which can be so helpful in teaching about expression and emotion, can take away the ability to focus. Most of us freely accept variety as a given and, if we are distracted by crooked teeth, a moustache or an oversized nose, we just look away or ignore it. If these issues draw your whole attention, they prevent focus on what is being said, explained or demonstrated. Now, it may be impossible to have a perfect face or to hide our appearance but we can offer support by not demanding eye contact and encouraging the individual to look to the side, reducing such distractions.

Aversion to a particular colour has been mentioned previously but in some cases the colours of walls, the clothing worn by a member of staff, the bold colours of the playground equipment or the colour of food can cause anxiety. Choose colours carefully for walls and furniture, opting for calming colours such as pale greens and blues that are recognised as 'easy on the eye' and avoiding intense colours such as red and bright orange. When an individual has an aversion to a specific colour to the point that coping is made difficult, consider whether it can be minimised – particularly in clothing, for example.

The clashing of colour and pattern can be something that many of us react to. Like other children we've mentioned, Sam loved *Thomas the Tank Engine* and, in an effort to please him, his parents decorated his room with a Thomas theme – from floor to ceiling. The wallpaper, the curtains, the light fixture, the duvet cover and the mat by the bed all celebrated this theme. Sam was not sleeping at night and his family were exhausted from the short nights. His mum asked his teacher whether she would come to assess their environment, and the bedroom, which had been so lovingly prepared for him, was recognised as the issue. As a result, the walls were painted in a calming pale blue. The curtains were altered to have a border of Thomas but were predominantly a plain colour. Similarly, the duvet was altered with a panel of Thomas across the bottom half. The light fixture and the floor mat remained the same. Sam responded well and his sleeping improved. His beloved Thomas was there to enjoy but not to overwhelm.

Auditory disturbance

> 'When I was a little kid I used to do stereotypical, repetitive behaviours, like sit for hours and dribble sand through my hands. Sometimes I rocked... I did this because loud sounds hurt my ears, so I did it to escape the loud sounds.'
> (Temple Grandin, 'The Best Life for Animals', 2009)

Even when it is quiet, we are surrounded by sound. We usually have the ability to block out the peripheral noises and focus on the main point, the individual speaking or the activity that we are involved in. For someone with hypersensitive hearing, the imperceptible sounds missed by others can disrupt or cause fear and anxiety. This, in turn, creates a distraction that impedes learning and participation.

These auditory sensitivities are frequently reported by individuals with autism. Certain sounds are perceived as more intense. For instance, frequencies can be extremely annoying (e.g. computer fan), loud noises can be painful (e.g. alarms or sirens) and combined sounds such as multiple people talking at once can be overwhelming. Dave, an adult with a PhD, supported the autism programme at a university. He explained the difficulty that he faced when talking in situations where other people were talking – pubs, shops, sports grounds, etc. Dave frequently had earphones in, listening to 'white noise' which calmed him in such situations – but it did make social discourse somewhat difficult!

In an educational setting, the hypersensitivity to a variety of sounds or frequencies can be challenging – even without the sounds of people, the computer fan, the projector for the interactive whiteboard, the heating system, the plumbing, chairs and tables moving on the floor, the click-clack of heels, the squeal of shoes, the intercom at the front door, the movement of vehicles in the car park, and textile on textile. Then add in the noises made by the people in the room, talking in a variety of pitches, tones and frequencies, the sound of the other children, and the noise that 'leaks' from the rest of the school and the wider environment. The use of ear defenders or noise-cancelling earphones does help some focus and improve attention.

Some children with autism make a variety of sounds, such as screams, moans, groans, growls or a range of other noises. These vocalisations often serve as a control, offering the child an element of camouflage to the sounds that fill their ears. It can, however, make the class setting a challenge. A young man in a generic special school was making life difficult for his peers due to deep-throated growling throughout the day. Both staff and children found this noise quite intimidating. Through trial and error, the staff found a noise that could be played through his Walkman™ that helped him to significantly reduce the intimidating growls. The idea actually came from a baby's sleep monitor, a low, rumbling frequency, resulting in significantly fewer incidents and a greater level of attention.

Hyposensitivity to auditory inputs can be overlooked as it does not always create the management difficulty that hypersensitivity can bring. The lack of response to the 'normal' range of sound can be mistaken for attention issues, social understanding difficulties and, sometimes, hearing loss. Joe (whom we met in Chapter 1) had a degree of hyposensitivity, initially labelled as hearing loss. Joe was generally not concerned by the noises around him – in fact, he was fascinated by the tone of American accents and could identify an American in a busy supermarket several aisles away! Ethan appeared to have no auditory sensitivities; sirens, bells and alarms would have no effect on him, resulting in him having to be physically prompted every time there was a fire alarm. He would, however, go into a significant meltdown at the sound of a baby crying, especially a newborn. Why this particular pitch? It is very hard to fathom but, once identified, supporting Ethan to cope with it was possible.

Jacob generally coped well within his mainstream classroom and was able to work alongside his peers throughout the day. On occasion he would begin to get very agitated and sometimes burst into tears. It took some time for him to explain that this happened when he heard a dog barking. No one else noticed this faraway sound but his fear of dogs coupled with hypersensitive hearing created a sense of danger for Jacob. His teacher worked with him to help him understand that he was in a safe setting: no dogs accessed the school grounds and the barking was just a sound in the distance. She involved the whole class in a listening game using pre-recorded sounds for them to identify. A range of familiar environmental sounds, including animals, created a fun session that helped Jacob to recognise the barking as one of many surrounding sounds.

At times, the sounds that create issues are very specific. Charles could not bear to hear anyone cough and when they did he became outraged. When his teacher had a dry throat and found it necessary to cough regularly, she explained, 'I'm sorry, Charles, I need to cough. Please be patient.' By addressing the issue, he responded and tolerated the situation. Oliver regularly let out a guttural sound during the day. Mia became distressed every time she heard the sound. Staff quietly reassured her, 'It's OK, it's just Oliver.' In a short period of time she accepted this and started to reassure herself with the same words. Leroy regularly disrupted

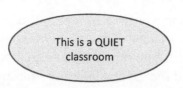

This is a QUIET classroom

Figure 4.2 *Classroom door poster*

the day by letting out a very high-pitched squeal, usually responding to the sound of footsteps in the corridor. In an attempt to manage this, he was encouraged to design a poster for the classroom door (see Figure 4.2).

On entering the room, Leroy was *consistently* reminded to read the poster, and the same message was visually displayed in the classroom and on his desk. A quiet symbol is often useful to reduce the noise level and support everyone within a setting, respecting the needs of those who require reduced volume and enabling a comfortable environment.

Blocking out environmental sounds can be a challenge. A group of students commented that they would be using 'the echoey room'. Having verbalised their dislike of this, they then helped to solve the problem by opening the window and door, thus improving the acoustic quality of the setting.

As mentioned previously, many individuals on the autism spectrum benefit from the use of ear defenders to reduce the distraction of sound. For some, this is rejected due to discomfort or not wanting to stand out, but having them available is a positive encouragement to using them as necessary. Having a few available for anyone in the group to use can reduce the stigma of being different.

> **Tip**
>
> Be alert! Watch for an individual covering their ears, putting their fingers in their ears, looking uncomfortable or retreating from the situation. Listen and attune your ears to what may simply be background noise for you – can you identify the reason?

Olfactory sensitivity

We all have reactions to odours, sometimes pleasant and enjoyable, while at other times revolting and repulsive. We literally and figuratively 'hold our nose' to block out unpleasant smells and often breathe in deeply to prolong those that we react positively to.

The impact of the sense of smell on self-regulation, behaviour and socialisation is frequently overlooked and some of the issues attributed to other senses. This sense can have a very significant impact on eating, diet and the sense of taste. Some of the dietary difficulties and issues that people with autism encounter are directly related to smell.

We often dismiss odours very quickly – pleasant ones with a smile and unpleasant ones with a scrunched-up nose! Tabitha's concentration diminished late in the morning and her teacher considered fatigue, low blood sugar and hunger, but eventually discovered that it was the smell of food being prepared in the school kitchen. This was a very difficult problem to overcome but this flexible teacher altered the class schedule to make this a more active time, focusing on concrete learning and highly motivating activities to distract from the offending smells.

A new purpose-built school had been designed with the vents for the kitchens next to the air circulation fans. Consequently, cooking and food smells were circulated around part of the school. This was difficult on many levels, but Nigel found it extremely challenging when fish in any form was being prepared. He would describe to his teacher that his head hurt and the smell would cause him genuine pain. The smell was actually very subtle, and for neurotypical staff and his hyposensitive peers it was not noticeable. Nigel had difficulties communicating verbally, making it difficult for him to describe how a smell could cause pain in the head. A common issue for those with sensory processing difficulties is explaining an abstract concept – feelings, sounds, tastes, smells, etc. – and communicating the hyper or hypo impact that they cause. Nigel's hypersensitive olfactory issues became more and more pronounced as he went through puberty and adolescence. He eventually began wearing a mask when in the community with his parents. They lived near a large bread factory and within 'smelling' distance of a brewery. His difficulties became so severe that he wouldn't venture out, his mask only providing a placebo effect. A creative-thinking care assistant came up with the idea of making use of a very mild essential oil under his nose – through some trial and error he actually found rosemary oil to be pleasant and effective, making life more bearable.

Hypersensitivity is difficult, and when coupled with hyposensitivity, further issues arise. Andy was a 'typical' teenage boy in many ways, disliking any attempts at bathing or showering, disliking haircuts and preferring dark clothing. Andy had a diagnosis of Asperger's and was coping at his local secondary school. He had hypersensitivity to bright light (which is why he grew his hair long, he reported) and hyposensitivity to his own smell. This was causing increasing difficulty at home and at school, due to his rather pungent body odour. He was completely unaware of it and it was a challenge to get him to take on board the impact of his odour on his family and peers. Eventually, through the engagement of Child and Mental Health Services, an autism-friendly dermatologist provided an acceptable solution. The challenge of sensory sensitivities, both hyper and hypo, is well illustrated with Andy's issues: hypersensitive about the feeling of water on his skin, in particular from a shower, and hyposensitive to smells, particularly his own. Combining this with theory of mind difficulties and complex social language usage demonstrates how challenging situations can become.

An important function of the sense of smell is its involvement in eating, from food selection to appreciation and recognition. Eating is a complex mechanism that involves three main variables: the eater (each with our own food history and sensations), the object (different food and its own particular characteristics) and the context (physical and social environment). Eating has generally become a far more complex process over the course of evolution, in particular, over the last 50 to 100 years. Eating well or 'normally' can be learned. The development of children's diet involves sensorimotor, social and psychological skills, and the whole process can be difficult; eating disorders in its widest meaning can affect many neurotypically developing children, but affects significantly more children with autism.

There are times when individuals with autism are overcome by the smells around them and find it impossible to ignore or dismiss them. This, in turn, leads to discomfort and distraction, sometimes inhibiting the ability to focus and concentrate. Chris had a very acute sense of smell and began to react negatively to a member of staff who, in his words, 'reeked of bacon' in the morning. His negative reaction and inability to participate in sessions were having an impact on his learning. But this staff member loved her bacon! A discussion on the issues led to her having breakfast before she showered and dressed, eliminating the odour from her hair and clothes. The flexibility of staff goes a long way to supporting the needs of individuals with sensory issues.

Javed was never seen to reject odours but had an absolute fascination with aromas that he enjoyed. For example, he would try to nestle his nose in people's hair and sniff deeply, with sheer delight on his face. Scented shampoo, any scent, provided a moment of pleasure. The difficulty with this was that, while family and school staff may have been tolerant of this, it is not acceptable to the general public and needed to be discouraged. Consistency is so important – every individual needed to respond in the same way in order to change the pattern. In this case, the simple statement 'No sniffing hair, Javed' was used, with moving away as he approached. By providing mini bottles of some of his favoured scents, Javed had times during the day when he could enjoy them without invading personal space. Other individuals, however, find the smell of some perfumes, body spray, aftershave and deodorants very unpleasant and distracting. Reducing their use or choosing unscented products is a small sacrifice to alleviate these issues.

It is not uncommon for mealtimes, whether in a school or a place of work, to create discomfort through the mixture of odours that permeate the space. Adults can often remove themselves from the situation by going out for lunch or for a walk. In a school context it is much more difficult, and creative solutions need to be found to eliminate the stress that results – perhaps eating a packed lunch in a quiet classroom or in a designated area distanced from the serving hatch?

Camden's parents were concerned because he was refusing to use the toilets at school. He would be bursting when he arrived home and sometimes did not make it to the toilet. Discussing it with the school, it became evident that the problem was related to the odour of the toilets. This is not an easy situation to alter unless it is purely related to the cleaning products being used. In this case, that was not at the heart of the matter. It was an old school building and it seemed impossible to mask the smells without causing this response from Camden. When staff put their heads together they found a solution. The disabled toilet was accessible and recently refurbished. Camden was introduced to this new arrangement and began to use it during the day.

> **Tip**
>
> The willingness of a school or workplace to be flexible and take sensory issues seriously meets the needs of both families and individuals on the autism spectrum.

Gustatory sensitivities

Delicious! Disgusting! Yummy! Yuck! We all have food favourites and food that we reject. Taste is a very personal thing. Many individuals with autism have aversions to or love of particular tastes. It's worth noting that food choices are not just based on flavour or strength of taste but can also be related to the texture of the food.

For example, Nathen would not eat anything green. His parents attributed this to his first encounter with green food – peas. He spat them out and from that moment on, nothing green touched his lips. In some ways this may not be a problem worth fighting over, but by introducing pieces of a peeled green apple and Nathen loving it, bits of the skin were left on until he began to eat it unpeeled and then gradually accepted other green foods, such as grapes and cucumber. Small steps, no pressure, led to desensitising his aversion.

The sense of taste is obviously closely related to the sense of smell; the interrelatedness of the two is well documented. There is increasing evidence from parents and the autistic population that response to both taste and smell is atypical; anecdotally, these responses are frequently extreme. Harry could not tolerate any foods that had a strong taste, which was very problematic, with his dietary intake based on beige – bland cereals, mashed potatoes, few vegetables or fruit except Golden Delicious apples or bananas, rice, very processed sausages and the standard McDonald's®. He would not tolerate strong, sour, salty or sweet flavours and struggled with strong smells like coffee, curry or vinegar. Harry had sensorimotor issues and would continually chew on clothes, pens, plastic and LEGO®, a particular favourite. At the time, it was challenging to find appropriate compensatory interventions, unlike the present day, when there are numerous 'chewies' available that are very appropriate! Samson was the polar opposite of Harry, eating extremely strongly flavoured foods, including curries, chillies, gravy made with lots of granules, and toast that was very well done and slathered with Marmite®. Samson would crave these strong flavours and at home cupboards had to be locked after he had eaten a whole jar of curry powder and, on another occasion, a jar of coffee (medical advice was sought here, due to the amount of caffeine he ingested). Samson had 'pica' (a disorder that is characterised by eating things in the environment that are generally inedible). He had a particular taste for cigarette ends and he was able to spot a discarded cigarette at some distance. Pica does have a sensory aspect, but it will be discussed further in Chapter 5.

We discussed Sally in previous chapters. Sally had a very restrictive diet and at times of stress this would become even more restricted. Reflecting back over 20 years, it is clear that very little thought was given to the sensory aspect of Sally's needs. Sally was perhaps hyposensitive to taste, yet had other aspects of her sensory processing that were clearly hypersensitive – the benefit of hindsight clarifies issues of the past.

Snacks at school can be an interesting window on likes and dislikes. Knowing the right shade of toast is a challenge, from warm bread with no colour to not acceptable until the smoke is rising. Micah ate one brand of white bread and could recognise a sneaky substitute at 20 paces! Amber insisted on the exact thickness of a popular yeast extract food spread, and it was a generous portion. Jack, on the other hand, had to be seated a distance from Amber to avoid the sight and smell of her toast.

Dinnertime at school creates the challenges of children eating only soft food (mash, yogurt, well-cooked pasta…) or only crispy food (chips, nuggets, crackers…) or only pink foods or only white foods or only... you get the picture! The challenges of generalising and the reluctance to accept change can play havoc with nutrition and a range of acceptable foods.

Finding ways to expand the menu is a challenge that needs to be addressed. Slowly and surely it is possible to entice an individual to try something new. Being creative in planning simple cookery sessions and tasting sessions that are delivered in a relaxed and enjoyable way can encourage tasting without the pressure of mealtime. Will it always be successful? No, but when success occurs it makes a difference to the wellbeing of the individual. In one such session, the group were making fruit salad, learning to identify fruits, pare and cut. The final product was shared and each child tasted – success! Until Basil consumed his chosen fruit and 'frisbeed' the bowl and remaining contents across the room! In spite of the clean-up, the overall activity and outcomes were positive.

Pica, as mentioned previously, can be a real issue and requires careful monitoring and vigilance. Sean particularly sought out plastic carrier bags to shred and ingest, a potentially dangerous obsession. It was imperative that everyone involved in his care took precautions to eliminate the bags. He would sometimes pick up metal objects such as nuts and bolts, and before he could be intercepted they would be swallowed. Trips to A&E were all too frequent from both home and school. Sean's cognitive ability made it very difficult for him to understand the implications of his actions, putting the onus of responsibility on the adults caring for him. More common materials that need to be monitored are paint, glue, paper and crayons, making supervision of activities a necessity, while consistently pointing out the inedible nature of tempting objects.

Tactile issues

Tactile issues take on many forms, including the fear of certain textures and substances as well as the aversion to being touched. This has implications for crowded spaces, standing in queues, being brushed against when peers walk by and the well-meaning friendly hugs of others. If 'sticky fingers' are an aversion, are they necessary? Does everyone have to finger-paint or work with clay? Can a child be last in the queue to avoid being shuffled by others? Some solutions are really quite easy to offer in reducing discomfort.

The sense of touch is far more than simply feeling with our hands. It also involves any sensation related to our skin-covered bodies. Tactile defensiveness is a hypersensitivity to touch. Parents of children with autism and adults with autism have reported that they find their skin is extremely sensitive to everyday things, including some fabrics and clothes, or brushing or combing hair. This may be presented by the inability or reluctance to wear specific clothing, frequently woollen garments or 'slippy' materials like nylon or silk. Socks, particularly the seams, and shoes – too tight, not tight enough or rubbing or slipping – can create discomfort, and these feelings are often exacerbated when the person is under stress. Phil would attempt to strip his clothes off if he was at all stressed or if demands were too great. His father told us that the first thing he did when he came home from school was to completely strip and wrap himself in his duvet. A young man who had Asperger's told me about the pain that the labels in his shirt would cause him; he had a good job in accountancy so had to wear a formal suit and tie, and he would immediately remove the label in the collar and the washing instructions on new shirts. Every evening after his commute home, he would need to spend at least an hour naked in his bedroom before donning baggy cotton pyjamas. For each of these individuals, they had developed coping strategies.

Typically developing children learn a great deal through messy play: finger painting, wet or dry sand – all sorts of 'sensory' play goes on in nursery and Reception classes. Someone with tactile defensiveness finds these experiences extremely problematic, often rejecting them. It is not uncommon for autistic individuals to have an aversion to resources that are commonly enjoyed. In schools, salt dough, shaving foam, gloop, finger paints, etc. are seen to be fun and serve many purposes, including early symbol-making. Hugo couldn't tolerate anything on his hands and avoided the range of materials available for exploration. A balance was struck by providing dried lentils, rice and pasta to encourage him to engage with his peers and explore materials. Farouk was struggling at his nursery, refusing to go into the 'messy' room and attempting to run away from it. Eventually he began to tolerate entering the room wearing protective clothing, but would not entertain paint, gloop or cooked pasta experiences. Farouk also had an extreme reaction to rain, a difficult challenge to avoid in Manchester! With the support of his occupational therapist, many of his anxieties around wet and messy things were reduced.

Touching with our hands can be both a pleasant experience and one to be avoided. Saria was anxious at school and often wept silent tears. When her mother brought her to school it was noticed that Saria stroked her mother's headscarf. Her teacher brought a number of silky scarves to school and every morning Saria ran them through her fingers and chose one to carry with her, often stroking it. This comforting tactile experience settled her and renewed her spirit.

Hypo- or hypersensitivity to pain is an extreme aspect of sensory processing. Joe was introduced in Chapter 1 and is an example of being hyposensitive in many respects. His reaction to pain was atypical. If he fell in the yard at breaktimes or out playing, there was little or no reaction. When visiting a soft play centre, he broke his arm at some stage but it was three days before his parents took him to A&E as he had never complained but they recognised that something was not right. When his arm was in a cast, he continued with his games and played as though nothing had happened. What may have been overlooked was Joe's level of arousal when he hurt himself; he was very excited and happy at the soft play centre, and usually Joe was similarly excited at breaktimes and running around – the power of natural endorphins to overwhelm the pain receptors is perhaps one explanation.

Hyposensitivity to touch helps to explain why some individuals with autism do not feel cold and hot in their extremes. Sophie never felt the need to wear her jacket, no matter how cold the day. Bryan wore his hooded jacket all year round, even in unbearable heat. Elinor burnt herself on a wall heater but expressed no pain, and the injury was only discovered when she changed for PE. The burn was extensive, requiring professional treatment.

Ewan was at the other end of the sensory scale. He attended a mainstream primary and was fully included in school life. However, Ewan's reactions were having an impact on his relationships with others. If another pupil walked past him, barely brushing his arm, for example, his reaction could be extreme, as if he had been severely injured. This began to have a detrimental effect on how his peers viewed him. Hypersensitivity and tactile defensiveness were a significant feature of Ewan's autism – he was a 'fussy' eater, disliked art and messy activities and would get terribly distressed if his clothes were dirty or wet. These issues were reflected at home and were causing the family some difficulty. A referral to occupational therapy and careful assessment of Ewan's responses resulted in giving him 'heavy work'; he was given a weighted vest and had a weighted blanket at night. These interventions made a significant impact on Ewan's level of arousal and, consequently, a noticeable reduction in his tactile defensiveness. One unforeseen but pleasant 'side effect' of the occupational therapy input was Ewan's reaction to kisses from his mother! He had previously wiped them off as they 'stung' but he began to tolerate and eventually accept the physical shows of affection from his mum.

It is not uncommon for hair-cutting to be described as painful and can be avoided at all costs. This can be a nightmare for parents who like orderly hair – although not a problem to the individual who is happy to let it grow and grow. In support of parents, some schools have made it a point to desensitise children by using combing and brushing hair as part of relaxation sessions. Some have even provided an 'in-house' hairdresser who, through small steps and building relationships with students, has their approval to cut and style hair. Similarly, brushing teeth can be an obstacle to hygiene and is an area where home and school can work together. One school gradually exposed their pupils to the sensation, the taste, etc. and then shared consistent practice and resources with home. One parent commented that he had never been successful in getting his son to brush his teeth whereas he now did this three times a day, voluntarily.

As mentioned earlier, touch is a whole-body experience. Hannah flinched every time that anyone brushed past her. The slightest touch felt painful. Martin wore clothes that were a larger size than necessary so that they were loose on his torso. Lili's dad had to remove all tags from clothing due to the discomfort that they caused. On the other hand, deep pressure can bring comfort and is part of the sensory diets (described on page 90) provided for some individuals with autism.

Tip

Hats off to those who seek to identify the issues that individuals with autism are struggling with, take them seriously, look for creative solutions and implement them!

Vestibular – the sense of balance and stability

The vestibular sense is related to movement or balance, receiving sensory messages from an organ in the middle ear. This responds to head and body movement related to direction and speed. Being hypersensitive to vestibular stimulation causes reactions to ordinary movement activities, such as swings, slides, ramps and inclines. Other difficulties include learning to climb or descend stairs or hills, and apprehension about walking or crawling on uneven or unstable surfaces. Children may literally trip over their own feet, bounce off walls or fall out of chairs. Previously, these difficulties were sometimes mistaken for dyspraxia or interpreted as 'clumsy'. These issues can create inactivity and reluctance to participate in games, PE or outdoor activities. Sitting posture deters from handwriting and presentation skills. Andy, previously mentioned in this chapter, had difficulties with vestibular processing, resulting in poor coordination and posture. He used creative ways to avoid activities that involved coordination or movement, which further excluded Andy from his peers. Access to an occupational therapist qualified in 'sensory integration' could have addressed many of his issues.

Hyposensitivity within the vestibular realm is exemplified by Michael, who would balance on the very top of the climbing frame, causing staff to take a sharp intake of breath. Arjun would swing without holding on, beyond what is considered safe. They were both seeking input into their vestibular sense. Many will spin, flap or rock to get that missing sensation, finding it hard to be still, as their vestibular system gives mixed or confusing feedback. Grounding activities such as heavy digging, wall pushes or deep pressure may offer the feedback needed. An occupational therapist trained in sensory integration is a godsend for identifying specialist equipment such as bespoke seating and peanut or therapy balls. The work is aimed at strengthening and developing gross motor skills (people with vestibular problems tend to have low muscle tone), including exercises that encourage 'crossing the midline': using the left hand and arm on the right side of the body and vice versa. Specialist therapy rooms provide a variety of swings or hammocks, crawl tubes or Lycra® tunnels. A much more holistic approach to the sensory needs of the pupils and students, based on individualised assessment and evaluation, is without doubt best practice.

Proprioceptive – self-movement and body position

The proprioceptive sense uses feedback from muscles and joints, identifying where our body is in space and what forces are acting on it. An individual may have gravitational insecurity and become anxious to take their feet off solid ground, like when climbing or using the toilet. If you are walking, for example, you don't look at your feet; you just know where they are and where they are going because you're receiving information from your proprioceptors in the muscles and joints of each limb. You receive constant information about muscle stretch, joint loading and compression, and how open or closed joints are. This sense identifies how much force you are using and whether you are carrying or pushing anything.

When seeking proprioceptive feedback, you may jump, crash, chew and mouth objects, enjoy 'hanging' or you may push objects or people. If you have a slow response to proprioceptive input, you may use too much force, frequently breaking things; you may have poor muscle tone and use too little pressure; or you may slouch or lean on people or objects. Proprioception informs the pressure for holding pens and pencils, with implications for writing or tapping a keyboard either too much or not enough. Ivan had some significant issues with his proprioception and, in particular, how to assess how much pressure to apply – he frequently put pencils through the page and painting was difficult. A very stark example can be illustrated through a farm visit. The children were allowed to stroke and handle rabbits, lambs and other small animals. The highlight was the chicks, which were a day or so old. Unfortunately, Ivan's proprioception meant that he did not understand 'gently' and he squashed the chick. Ivan found the whole incident very distressing and these issues persisted throughout over time. His hypersensitivity created other difficulties in school, with him frequently dropping things and struggling with the concept of personal space, often causing him to be upset. The occupational therapist worked hard to find interventions that would help both his proprioception and his level of self-regulation. As he was hypersensitive, the goal was to find strategies to reduce this sensitivity and lower his level of arousal to improve self-regulation. Some success was found through introducing a weighted vest and tight-fitting fingerless gloves, but even these had relatively limited impact overall.

Tip

The 'Alert' programme is a system developed by occupational therapists that aims to address the sensory input for children who have significant sensory processing difficulties. Using an analogy that the brain is an engine – too high revs and you are hyper, too low revs and you are hypo – the aim is to get your 'engine' running smoothly. By using the engine analogy to teach self-regulation (changing how alert we feel), the programme aims to help children to learn what to do if they are in a non-optimal state of alertness. The 'Alert' programme teaches children that there are five ways to change how alert they feel: put something in their mouth, move, touch, look or listen.

Interoception – what's happening inside

Perhaps the biggest issue with sensory processing is making sense of the inputs and identifying hypo or hyper. Is the sensation related to touch? Sound? Smell? And how do you describe the 'feelings' if you have communication difficulties? It gets even more complex and potentially challenging if you then take 'interoception' into account. Interoception is the sense that helps you to understand what is happening inside your body: hunger, thirst, the need to go to the toilet, etc. There are receptors that send information about the inside of your body to your brain. This helps to regulate vital functions like body temperature, hunger, thirst, digestion and heart rate. Interoception helps you to understand and feel what's going on inside your body. For instance, you know whether your heart is beating fast or you need to breathe more deeply. You're able to tell if you need to use the bathroom. You know whether you're hungry, full, hot, cold, thirsty, nauseated, itchy or ticklish. Additionally, our emotions have a physical manifestation within our bodies – fear makes our heart beat faster and excitement gives us a tickle in our tummy (butterflies!). These physical responses to emotions are also connected to the interoception receptors. Without clearly feeling and understanding these physical sensations, it is difficult to identify emotions with any degree of clarity. When our interoceptive system is properly working, the sensations alert us that our internal balance is off and it motivates us to take action – to do something that will restore the balance and help us to feel more comfortable. For example, if we feel thirsty, we get a drink; if we feel full, we stop eating; if we feel anxious, we seek comfort.

Our interoception system informs our actions, ensuring that internal balance is restored, providing that we understand the internal messages. Javid was a young man with severe challenging behaviour who appeared to struggle with many aspects of his daily life. Looking at a functional analysis of his behaviours, a subtle pattern emerged – incidents of difficult behaviour were followed by a visit to the toilet and incidents were also noticed if he was stopped from eating. It could have been that Javid did not understand the internal signals – a full bladder could have been painful or cause him fear, and he may not have understood when he was 'full' and thought that he needed to keep eating. Matthew had such serious self-injurious behaviour that he had a callus forming on his forehead. There had been a great deal of functional analysis of Matthew's behaviours but to no avail, and it later turned out that he had a recurring ear infection that was not being treated, as no one knew. Matthew could not communicate his pain, if he even understood it. We can only speculate but perhaps it does give us another avenue to explore when dealing with unexplained behaviours. We are only just beginning to look at the interoceptive system and its relationship with autism. This is a potentially very exciting area of research.

Tip

Many behaviours commonly thought of as 'autistic', including toe walking, hand-flapping and rocking, can be attempts to deal with sensory integration dysfunction.

Bringing the senses to life

There are so many ways to support sensory issues and broaden tolerance and understanding, extend experiences and desensitise sensitivities.

Sensory stories

Sensory stories are created through the use of artefacts and actions to bring the story to life. One example we have seen is 'The Magic Carpet', using movement with a repeated rhyme, the aroma of spices, the tactile feel of ointments, the sound of a gong, musical accompaniment and a dragon puppet – the story was brought to life and the children were engaged. Resources were creatively chosen and supported by a wide range of visuals – sheer enjoyment! Another example focused on going to the seaside, wearing sun hats and sunglasses, spraying water and exploring the feel of sand with their feet.

Café days

College students benefited from a full sensory experience through running a monthly café for staff. Sensory experiences included the smells and tastes of preparing food, organising and navigating space, communication through menus, welcoming and writing orders, balancing trays and carrying dishes. In another school the focus was on Holland, and a variety of foods were introduced – cheese, sausage, breads, syrup waffles, etc. Pupils were encouraged to smell and taste each, widening their experiences and encouraging tolerance of new things.

Sensory passports

Also referred to as sensory profiles or personal learning plans, these are invaluable in outlining likes and dislikes relevant to individual needs. They include 'sensory barriers to learning', with a list of issues for each individual, e.g. 'does not like to hear others eating or see their mouths open'. Triggers are identified and strategies are provided, including reference back to visual support and arrangements for specific times of the day that are problematic. Outlining needs, such as time on a trampoline and swings, helps to prepare for returning to work. For one young woman, who explained that she enjoys physical contact, staff developed the term 'safe hugs' and encouraged her to use a ball or cushion to squeeze instead of adults. Hyper and hyposensitivities are also noted, with information on how this impacts on the pupil. Resources that benefit the young person are listed (see the examples on page 91). Drawing this information together, making it available to all staff supporting the individual and sharing this information with families and carers supports the wellbeing of the person with autism. The sensory passports can be written from the student's perspective and address individual needs, including 'What I know about myself' and then listing 'Things I like' and 'Things I don't like'. For example, one young person identified chewing, going barefoot, smelling things and playing with silly putty as likes, in contrast to disliking their hair being washed, heat, socks, high-pitched sounds and complete silence. The latter fits in with the 'white noise' present in some sessions through soft music.

Pupil context sheets also provide information to support sensory issues – for example, staff reminders such as 'make sure the room is not too hot or too cold as he is not able to say he is feeling uncomfortable'. Some classrooms have sensory 'charts' for each pupil identified with these issues. These include specific information on each of the senses as well as positive comments on what the child manages well. The charts inform behaviour documents on how the physical environment could be adapted to reduce stress – for instance, 'If I am feeling stressed I could ask to move away from the group or leave the room and go to a quiet area'.

Sensory diets

This has nothing to do with food! When sensory issues are highlighted, a menu of activities to work into the schedule to alleviate the impact can be very helpful. The diet outlines strategies to support specific issues, e.g. awareness of noise levels in different environments, building 'retreat' times into the day, exercise breaks, deep pressure, etc. Working with the individual to plan the appropriate diet is essential but responding spontaneously when the senses are overwhelmed is also necessary. Review and evaluation of the strategies to ascertain those most successful should be part of the system. Movement breaks and opportunities for relaxation are incorporated across the day to address the sensory needs of pupils. The sensory room and quiet withdrawal areas are used as necessary. One pupil had a prompt on his desk saying, 'Help me please, I need to go out'.

Sensory diets are used to 'retrain' the brain to accept sensory inputs in a more typical way; the idea is that through repetition, the young person's nervous system will respond in a more 'organised' way to sensations and movement. These sensory diets could include repetitive balance activities, increasing in their complexity, activities to improve muscle tone and tasks that could develop more 'organised' responses to sensory stimulation.

Sensory circuits

Many children who have a lengthy journey to school benefit from a well-organised circuit of exercise before they have to face the classroom. This may be a sports hall set out with defined areas that are labelled with words and/or symbols to identify the activity and order of rotation. The range of equipment is designed to prepare for learning, to stimulate and to relax.

For example, an observed session was led by a teaching assistant who calmly and confidently supported the pupil throughout. When bouncing on the exercise ball, she sang a song and then paused, waiting for him to sign 'more', and then continued. His face showed utter pleasure. On completion, key words were used for 'last time'. In keeping with the development of independence, he was asked to put his shoes on. When he did not respond, the occupational therapist (who had joined the session briefly) took off her own shoe, repeated the instruction and modelled the action. The child followed this and put his shoes on. This demonstrates the overlap of addressing sensory issues and supporting communication and attention.

Sensory resources

A wide range of sensory resources are available to support each of the senses. Their use needs to be evaluated to ensure that they are appropriate for the individual. They include squeeze vests, weighted blankets, Pilates balls, chewies, ear defenders, trampettes, swings, scooter boards, weighted blankets, shoulder wraps, wobble cushions, vibrating toys, ball chairs, small tactile objects, fabrics, etc. In one school, to encourage a pupil to accept a weighted vest that was assessed as a helpful resource, they purchased novelty ones based on police

Sensory impact

and firefighter themes. In another school where a child benefited from weight bearing, they let him choose a themed backpack that was filled with the assessed amount of sand and he went for calming walks when he became anxious (see the further reading section on page 157 for accessible resources).

Specialist areas

Providing appropriate spaces for relief from sensory overload or to create calm in the midst of busyness is often found in specialist environments. Examples are:

- a quiet room with soft furnishings and lighting
- a sensory garden with paths, seating areas and the aroma of herbs and plants
- a 'take five' room to let off steam
- quiet corners in classrooms
- fitness suites
- well-equipped outdoor areas with sensory-supportive equipment.

Tip

Sensory integration should not be an added extra but part of the routine across each day. It needs to be well planned for and based on a sound understanding of the specific needs of each individual. Being alert to the need for a break, providing a range of sensory equipment, auditing and modifying the environment, and committing to recognising the impact of the senses on daily life is essential to foster the wellbeing of individuals on the autism spectrum. Appointing a sensory 'guru' who is trained up to support other staff and parents in deciphering issues that may be rooted in the senses is well worth considering.

Sensory takeaways

- Audit the environment and consider its impact on sensory issues.
- Seek advice for sensory assessments and specialist support to provide individualised programmes.
- Recognise sensory barriers to learning and set targets to overcome them.
- Be a detective and look at incidents through your trusty magnifying glass.
- Be alert to both under- (hypo) and over- (hyper) sensitive responses.
- Find ways to build tolerance rather than eliminate every sensory issue.
- Develop a range of sensory resources to be made available as needed.
- Access training to create increased understanding of the breadth of sensory issues.

5 Behaviour: It's not just tantrums!

People with autism can and do present a range of behaviours that challenge. These behaviours occur across the spectrum; however, they may be more frequently expressed by people with autism and an additional learning difficulty. The most common definition of 'challenging behaviour' is those behaviours that are likely to cause significant harm or disruption or that may result in the person being excluded from 'everyday' activities and/or having a very significant negative impact on the person's quality of life (see www.challengingbehaviour.org.uk). In this chapter we will be addressing behaviours that result in others being hurt, self-injurious behaviours, destructive behaviours, eating inedible objects (pica), controlling behaviours and other behaviours that challenge, including smearing, spitting, running away and stripping. This list is by no means exhaustive but it contains the behaviours that most frequently result in external support and advice being sought.

Points to consider:

- Behaviour is an attempt to communicate.
- Anxiety is the common thread running through behaviours that challenge.
- These actions do not occur because the young person is necessarily misbehaving, attention-seeking or simply putting it on.
- The same observed behaviour may serve differing purposes at different times.
- Challenging behaviours can be prevented or reduced if the right kind of support is provided – support that is flexible and personalised to the needs of the individual and that individual's context.
- Understanding the behaviour can be the secret to reducing the challenge.

Why do these behaviours occur?

All behaviours will serve a purpose to the person exhibiting the behaviour and it is really important to remember this in the difficult times. It is important to bear in mind that most people without a learning disability would also have displayed challenging behaviour very early in their lives. These 'terrible twos' do not usually last, because most two-year-olds develop a range of communication and social skills that enable them to get what they want and need rather more easily. Children with autism do not always develop these skills; therefore they may not have an efficient and effective mechanism to get their needs and wants met.

People with autism can and do struggle to understand what is happening around them and feel that they have no control over what happens to them or that they are not enabled to make choices. A number of people with autism who exhibit self-injurious behaviours may have pain or discomfort as a result of underlying and/or undiagnosed physical problems, and as we have seen in the previous chapter, sensory processing difficulties can result in frustrations that may have a behavioural impact. Similarly, we have seen in previous chapters that change or unfamiliar situations cause anxiety, which in turn can result in difficult behaviours. Being asked to do more than they can cope with or being given a task that is too difficult, long or boring can potentially lead to 'outbursts'. Some people with autism may struggle if they cannot access a favoured toy or activity. If they are being bullied, this may result in more aggressive or withdrawn behaviours. People with autism can, like anyone, simply be tired, fed up or just having an off day.

Jason is thirsty. However, due to his lack of 'theory of mind', he does not know that we (his carers) do not know that he is thirsty. Jason therefore gets frustrated and exhibits some behaviours in an attempt to get his need for a drink met. Perhaps Jason is thirsty but, because of his sensory processing difficulties, he is not aware of the root cause of this uncomfortable feeling and he consequently 'acts out'. Or perhaps Jason is thirsty but cannot verbalise it, and water is not readily available, so he takes himself to where he knows that water is freely available (the toilet). You can see that difficult behaviours can arise through a number of issues; however, the underlying issue is straightforward – Jason is thirsty. Jason's 'behaviour that challenges' could be avoided if we drill down and look closely at the STAR analysis of the behaviours:

- **Settings:** Where was the young person, what was going on around them and who was there? Consider the context of the incident.
- **Trigger:** Was a demand made?
- **Actions:** Consider a detailed description of the behaviours.
- **Response:** What were the consequences immediately following the behaviours? (Clements and Zarkowska, 2000)

A key aspect when looking at behavioural issues in autism is the role of anxiety. Although anxiety is not yet considered a core feature of autism, anxiety disorders are the most common comorbid conditions. It is particularly important to recognise and treat anxiety in autism, since it has such an impact on all aspects of the disorder, exacerbating social withdrawal as well as repetitive behaviours.

Our neurotypical world can be a confusing place for those on the autism spectrum. They may find social or unfamiliar situations overwhelming and hard to understand. There can be difficulty in working out what another person might be thinking or feeling, or how that person may react. As a result, people and situations can seem unpredictable, which can cause stress and anxiety. On top of that, individuals with autism may have trouble telling you that they're feeling anxious. All of these issues may result in behaviours that challenge.

Hurting others and aggression

It can be difficult to have a conversation addressing aggression in people with autism; however, it is a fact of life for many families and people with autism. A study in *Research in Autism Spectrum Disorders* (Hill et al., 2014) states that one in four young people with autism show aggressive behaviours, such as hitting others, destroying property or throwing 'temper tantrums'. In this study, aggression was more common among autistic children with additional learning difficulties. Children with significant aggressive behaviour also tended to have mood and anxiety symptoms, and difficulty sleeping and paying attention. This often results in lashing out, frequently in moments of anger or frustration, and often at caregivers and family members. Obviously, this is a major source of stress for families.

Pat was a young man whose aggressive outbursts had led to permanent exclusion from several special schools and had eventually led him to a specialist residential school many miles from his home. Pat certainly had difficulties with his moods; his reactions to demands could be very unpredictable – one moment he would happily 'do his work' and in another he would 'explode', up-end furniture and 'attack' staff. His team became particularly adept at picking up signals – very small changes in his demeanour or expression – and intervening with a range of strategies, such as time out, relaxation techniques or walks in the grounds. The intervention that would make the most impact was working with Pat to recognise the internal signals himself. This work would be vital for Pat's future, but would be a very challenging task. Detailed functional analysis of the behaviour incidents, looking very carefully at the antecedents (what was going on before the incidents), the actual incident and then how everybody reacted or acted after the incident, were the starting points. Working with young people who exhibit behaviour that challenges must be seen as a marathon, not a sprint. When Pat left the residential school at 19, there was a significant improvement in the frequency and intensity of his behaviour. He was in a much better place himself, as the physical interventions had reduced markedly; however, the behaviours had not been completely extinguished. Reflecting back on the behaviours that Pat exhibited, his meltdowns and incidents could last for several hours and require up to eight staff at a time to ensure that everyone was kept safe. When Pat came out of the behaviour episode, the most important thing for him was to make sure that everyone else was OK – Pat was always sad and upset at his loss of control.

The intent behind the behaviours should never be lost; it is rare that there is any malicious intent or a deliberate personalised 'attack'. To be really secure in the underlying reason requires a great deal of analysis, objective thinking and real empathy with the young people. Take Stephan, for example: he was enjoying some time on the scooter during a break when Brenda got in his way, causing him to fall. His reaction was to run to the nearest member of staff – not for comfort but to bite her hand. It is not unusual for a child to retaliate through an adult rather than to the peer. It's safer! Calmness was retained and the member of staff, although feeling the pain, comforted Stephan. The following day, during outside play, Stephan approached the member of staff, gently took her hand and stroked it. This non-verbal child was offering understanding and an apology – words were not needed. Wayne provides another example of a similar type of behaviour – he would hit a member of staff if another pupil made a specific noise (the noise could be a precursor to a 'meltdown'). Wayne was very anxious around this pupil and was communicating his anxiety to the member of staff. The team provided Wayne with more appropriate 'escape' methods and the hitting reduced. Again, these examples show that anxiety appears to be the basis for many difficult behaviours. Through careful 'functional analysis' of the young person's behaviour, a more appropriate and acceptable form of communication may be found.

Difficult behaviours can also be 'used' to escape – escape from activities or demands that are too much for the young person. They are also a very effective means of securing something tangible (food, games or activities, or the TV remote, for example). Rewarding negative behaviours can give the wrong message, so it is important to develop more positive methods to achieve desired outcomes: praise when deserved and rewarding spontaneous positive behaviour.

Parents are very frequently the 'target' for hitting; this is most likely because parental love is unconditional and parental responses are predictable. However, hitting a stranger gets a very 'exciting' response. Jordan was a young lady whose complex behaviours had resulted in her attending a residential school. In the wider community (including her previous schools), she appeared to get unintentionally positive feedback from her inappropriate interactions – she got a buzz out of hitting and the immediate reactions of family or staff. It became increasingly challenging to take Jordan into the community, as her 'hitting' was rapidly becoming a social inclusion issue. Taking a very close and detailed look at Jordan and her day-to-day life, it was clear that her 'circle' was becoming smaller and smaller as her behaviours got more difficult. Was Jordan simply seeking interactions with others? With the support of occupational therapy, speech and language therapy, and psychology, Jordan's mum and others involved in her day-to-day care, a plan was developed that addressed Jordan's initiation and greetings, her over arousal and her reactions. Staff were prompted on how to respond to her more inappropriate behaviours and how to develop more appropriate interactions. The result of a great deal of hard work and patience from all, not least Jordan, was that she attended the local Guides group and she could go to the shops and make her own choices. Jordan just got her communication badly wrong and, given the appropriate tools and feedback, she flourished. This is a good example of the team approach to behaviour problems. Analysing Jordan's needs from all perspectives and consistently applying agreed interventions resulted in a very much improved quality of life.

Of course, it is not always 'happily ever after' and it can be extremely hard to extinguish extreme behaviour that challenges.

Low-level behaviours can be equally challenging. Anton rejected curriculum sessions and, when new concepts were being introduced, he needed the support of a teaching assistant. Unfortunately, during the side-by-side work he would, almost imperceptibly, pinch and twist any exposed flesh on the teaching assistant's arm. Emphasising 'gentle hand' was not successful and the only solution was for staff to wear protective arm shields. With the coverings, Anton received no positive feedback from the pinching and it stopped. After a period of time, the shields were removed and the pinching did not resume. The habit was broken. Of course, Anton was looking for 'something' when he was pinching, and whatever it was was replaced – staff were likely to be much more positive in working with Anton if they were not being pinched, and Anton would pick this up. Regardless of what has been written previously, children with autism can be empathetic!

It's important to remember that not all individuals on the spectrum exhibit behaviour that challenges, and there is an even smaller number of cases where the behaviour cannot be assumed to have the intention to deliberately hurt someone. There have been a number of cases reported in the media where someone with Asperger syndrome or 'high-functioning autism' has deliberately targeted someone. The diagnosis of Asperger syndrome and psychopathy, or a similar label, can significantly complicate the situation in the eyes of the media. The reality is that people with autism (in all its forms) are no more likely to be involved in crime than the general populace. They are, however, overrepresented in the criminal justice system; as a population, they are more vulnerable – the desire to have friends has led some autistic people to be befriended by criminals and become their unwitting accomplices. People on the autism spectrum often do not fully understand other people's motives. The issue of autism and the criminal justice system will be discussed further in Chapter 6.

Self-injurious behaviours (SIB)

Self-injurious behaviour or SIB is where a person physically harms themselves. This may be head-banging on floors, walls or other surfaces, hand- or arm-biting, hair-pulling, eye-gouging, face- or head-slapping, skin-picking, scratching or pinching, or forceful head-shaking. According to an article published in *Brain Sciences* (Summers et al., 2017), up to 50 per cent of autistic people may engage in SIB at some point in their life, and it may affect people of all ages.

Why this extreme behaviour happens is frequently multifactorial. Matthew, whom we met earlier, had a large callus on his forehead as a result of his head-banging; he had a recurring inner ear infection that must have caused significant pain. When doctors finally sorted the issue, his extreme head-banging reduced significantly and eventually disappeared. A very significant number of people with autism and a learning difficulty appear to have an underlying medical issue that causes pain and/or discomfort.

Leon had autism with severe learning difficulties and suffered from a late-onset seizure disorder. After a number of seizures, he started to severely punch and hit himself on the head. This became extremely serious and resulted in several inpatient stays in hospital, as he was causing himself serious injury and negative long-term consequences. Leon had a very complex seizure disorder and neurologists were struggling to find drugs that would help; it took a great deal of time to find the combination of drugs that improved both his seizures and his SIB. Over a period of several years and placements in both psychiatric hospitals and specialist children's services, eventually his orthotic head protection could be taken away and the quality of Leon's life significantly improved. Leon's mum is convinced that his seizures were causing a very uncomfortable 'brain fuzz' that made Leon feel confused and scared, and it was this that was the cause of his self-injurious behaviours. Leon didn't have the communication skills to explain. He was not in control and had no method of expressing what was happening to him internally. The feelings of having no control, not being listened to and feeling unwell are reported as being potential reasons for self-injury.

Manuel reacted to seeing his reflection and would head-butt the surface where it appeared. Mirrors can be removed, stainless and reflective surfaces can be avoided but it is impossible to eradicate window glass. This posed a huge problem for Manuel and those supporting him at home, school and in the community. Anxiety increased this pattern and vigilance was essential. Distraction, playful interaction and careful consideration of seating, walking past shops, etc. were part of a continual risk assessment. Over time, the incidents reduced but the danger of injury remained whenever tension grew. Anxiety, again, played a very significant role in a very difficult behaviour episode.

When Tim became agitated he started to bang his head on the wall. His teacher took his hands and modelled taking a deep breath. Tim did the same. This was repeated several times and he calmed. The importance of finding a method of reducing stress and anxiety can allow the root of the behaviour to be found. To eradicate the head-banging, a more appropriate method of releasing tension and anxiety needed to be found – this is a long process and it is rare that there are successful quick fixes to behaviours that challenge.

In another example, a young person was skilfully distracted from SIB through encouraging a favoured activity (posting) to refocus and relax. Modelling, distracting and diverting can all be successful when relationships have been established and trust has been built. This is only possible when there is a thorough understanding of the individual's needs and complexities and when established interventions are **consistently** followed.

The National Autistic Society (2020) states that people who self-injure often report that this behaviour can be a reaction to anxiety after doing something wrong – it is very rarely a good idea to reprimand for self-injury. Being actively involved in choice-making and having a voice in decision-making reduces the frustration that can lead to SIB. It is vital to really look at what is going on in the person's life; whether it is at school, at home, in the workplace or in a residential placement, the SIB can be a reaction to something in the setting that staff and/or parents miss. SIB can be frequently anxiety-driven, can be the result of not being able to communicate easily or readily, and may be the result of interactions with others or a feeling of not being in control. It is vital to prevent the behaviour from becoming habitual, and external support (such as CAMHS) should be sought as soon as possible.

Destructive behaviour

Lucille's reaction to displays, particularly anything where paper was used, was to immediately grab and rip! This behaviour is very frustrating for those who have carefully enhanced the environment by mounting and double-mounting pieces of work and information for display. Books were also a target for Lucille on a daily basis. Now, consider Chapter 4 and the issues related to the senses. Lucille loved the sound of ripping paper! She was like a child in a sweet shop when it came to anything new and inviting. Once the issue was understood, she was provided with an ever-ready container of scrap paper and rewarded with shredding on completion of her work and as a choice activity. Lucille continued to be attracted to displays and books but a more appropriate behaviour had replaced the less acceptable and, as a bonus, the books were now displayed on higher shelves and provided the need for communication by pupils to access them. Protecting the displays under clear plastic reduced Lucille's desire to rip and hear the tearing sound but allowed the pupils access to their displayed work.

Bruce would, on a regular basis, destroy the TV or the glass hob that was in the kitchen of his home. He would be devastated when he did this, as food was very important to him and TV was his major interest. In this situation it is really hard to see the purpose behind his behaviour – it really seemed that he couldn't help these impulses or compulsions. The destruction was having a serious impact on his quality of life, as he became so distressed when he did it. His mother's natural reaction to seeing her son so distressed was to comfort him and reassure him that it would be OK and the item would be replaced. Perhaps this was the root of Bruce's behaviour. For a whole variety of reasons, Bruce may have needed his mother's attention and didn't know how to communicate this or may simply have been frustrated by the lack of daily comfort from his mum. The local social care service put into place a change of cooker (somewhat obvious but…) and gave Bruce a tablet that allowed daily video calls with his mum, as well as being more robust for personal TV. His communication system was completely overhauled and the behaviours significantly reduced. Sometimes the answer is obvious, but we need to step back to see it.

Bilal was the gifted artist we met earlier. If he was not drawing or painting tigers he would rip up his piece. He could be coaxed into attempting other subjects; however, he would rip on completion, oblivious to the quality of the work or of the effort he had put in. But when he was going in for a GCSE, he had to have a range of work to produce a portfolio. His teaching assistant and art teacher came up with the plan of buying Bilal's finished works. He would pass over the painting or drawing in exchange for some money to spend in the shop next to the school. This affirmation and reward saved the day!

Repetitive behaviours such as excessive straightening are commonly observed among individuals with autism. Attempts to prevent these behaviours may increase the likelihood of other problem behaviours. Arthur would spend a significant amount of time in the book corner trying to straighten and bring about order (as he saw it!). The difficulty was that books are not always the same size and if Arthur was at all dysregulated he would very quickly become extremely frustrated and trash the book corner and many of the books. It was agreed by all working with Arthur that he 'needed' to order things to help him regulate himself. A creative solution was found with the assistance of the school caretaker and the technology teacher. Arthur would sort and organise the tools, the wood and all the screws and nails. Gradually Arthur recognised that when he was stressed he could ask for a short period in the 'store' and he could regulate his anxiety. It was interesting that Arthur made no attempt to use this to escape from class work or other unfavoured activities, particularly assembly.

A school that catered for the needs of some very challenging youngsters who had PDA (pathological demand avoidance) behaviours, and would frequently destroy classrooms, bedrooms or the possessions of others, managed to significantly reduce this behaviour by actively involving the young people in the decoration, the choice of furniture and other aspects of daily living. Ownership seemed to reduce destructive behaviours, and creative use of outdoor space enabled the young people to self-manage their anxiety, stress and related arousal. For more information about PDA, see page 134.

Destructive behaviour can frequently, but not always, be related to feelings of not being involved, not being enabled to make personal choices and not understanding the demands being placed on the young people.

Pica

Pica refers to the eating of inedible objects and items from the environment, such as stones, leaves, cigarette ends, soil, hair or litter. The reasons can be medical, behavioural, sensory or a combination of these.

Sahel had autism, a severe learning difficulty and a diagnosis of pica. Sahel had visited hospitals on numerous occasions following ingestion of a range of items. He was extremely quick when he spotted something that he needed to eat. Sahel's family had had a long struggle to get pica identified as a specific diagnosis; paediatricians and medics saw it as just part of his wider condition. However, it was clear that Sahel's care team understood his pica and that for him, it appeared to be a sensory need and compulsion that made him happy and could calm him in times of anxiety. Clinical psychologists and the team around Sahel developed a range of interventions, including offering a wide and diverse range of 'chewies' with a range of shape, texture and hardness. His diet included extremes of bland foods and very strong flavours, such as Marmite® and hot curries. He was also given something to carry, which simply made his picking things up much harder. The pica was never eradicated but it did become more manageable and, thankfully, visits to hospitals reduced significantly.

Anecdotally, pica appears to be worse during times of stress or anxiety, and it would seem that finding more appropriate interventions to self-regulate is beneficial. The days of giving patients cigarettes in long-stay institutions may thankfully have passed, but we still have a responsibility to find acceptable and appropriate methods to meet the need that pica fills.

Pica should NEVER be seen as a 'safe behaviour', and needs to be viewed with the utmost seriousness. Ingestion of non-nutritive or non-food items can and has led to death.

Other behaviours – spitting, smearing, running away and stripping

Morgan was a young man with complex autism, requiring one-to-one support and very individualised learning. He was friendly and responsive, enjoying a range of concrete activities and sensory play. Morgan often spat at staff and generally at anything. This is often a difficult issue for staff to deal with, and regular changes of clothes were necessary. Through observation it became evident that Morgan had a regular build-up of saliva, known as hypersalivation. By clipping a towel to his waistband and showing him how to wipe his mouth, he was very happy to deal with the problem in this new way. The spitting was not aggressive; it was purely ridding himself of unwanted saliva.

Spitting is not an infrequent behaviour that parents and carers report as extremely challenging to deal with. Unfortunately, but not at all surprisingly, it is extremely difficult not to react to being spat at. This reaction may reinforce the behaviour, making it harder to extinguish or change. When assessing any challenging behaviour, it is vital to look closely at the function. Morgan's spitting was relatively straightforward, but it is not always so. Spitting could be sensory in its basis; it can be seen that, developmentally, young people will play with their saliva and experiment with spitting – if they get a good reaction, then the behaviour can quickly become entrenched. Spitting may be very effective at communicating 'leave me alone' or 'go away'. It may be that spitting is symptomatic of some dental issues going on – wobbly teeth, toothache, etc. Making a best guess at the root cause of the behaviour allows interventions to be developed. A young man placed in an adult service was given strong mints to eat when he started spitting. This really helped with his spitting; however, it masked an underlying reflux issue, which is why medical or dental investigations should be the starting point. An occupational therapist may suggest chewies or straws as alternatives, or apples and other healthier options could replace the mints. And try as hard as possible not to react!

Jin had autism and severe learning difficulties; he was non-verbal and was a very affectionate and tactile young man. This created some issues for staff. Jin had a 'habit' of smearing his faeces. At school this was thankfully quite infrequent, while at home it was a major issue. In his early teens, Jin remained doubly incontinent and was in pads during the day. Smearing is impossible to ignore and, however much you play down the incident, it is exceptionally hard to deal with. The first step was to ensure that Jin had no underlying medical issue. He was very constipated and this caused problems, so his diet was changed and this alleviated part of the problem. A sensory replacement was also sought and his team allowed him a very wide range of sensory experiences. Jin was developmentally young and needed many of the experiences that a toddler would experience. Smearing reduced but never fully went away. Jin's other difficult behaviour was regurgitation of his food, which was another significant challenge, not least because it could cause serious medical issues in later life. It is also hard to eradicate. The change to his diet to aid his constipation also helped slightly in his regurgitation; the use of chewies and very strong flavours helped as well. Neither behaviour went away fully, and sometimes a reduction is the best possible outcome.

There are aspects of behaviour that create danger for children with autism, and appropriate measures need to be put in place to keep individuals safe. The seeming need to run, to escape, is one of these. Secure buildings and perimeters are often required to ensure that danger is minimised while, at the same time, teaching road safety and stranger danger and providing clear boundaries. Louise liked to wander and her mother was constantly alert to the danger that this could cause. Doors at home were locked and keys were out of sight. One very early morning, Louise's mum received a telephone call from a neighbour, informing her that Louise had come over their back fence and injured herself. She had actually clambered over three other fences before reaching this particular garden. Fortunately, she was not seriously injured, but the security issues required rethinking. This is an example of try and try again to alter a behaviour that can be catastrophic if not addressed.

One autism-specific school had invested in some secure fencing to keep the children and young people safe, as there was a major road close by. The architects assured the school that the fences were 'climb proof' and proven in use at young offender institutions. However, within a week of opening with the children, a young lad scaled the fence with no problem – it wasn't secure for a determined young boy who wanted to see the sheep! The vigilance of staff is essential in spite of barriers or fences.

Joey was an older teenager who was kept in for his safety, both at school and at home. He just wanted to run and, ideally, have some member of staff chase him. He had no sense of danger and no road sense, and appeared to have no sense of direction. At every opportunity Joey would run; he thought that it was all a big game and would happily drop a basket in the supermarket and sprint out of the door if he saw half a chance. There had been several close calls: once Joey had escaped from his school when a delivery man was buzzed through, and he was straight off down the road, resulting in several hours searching and a police helicopter to track him down and get him back safely. After this, the rigorous risk assessment made it a challenge to find a safe way of accessing the community. Joey's significant risk was reducing his opportunities for socialisation and for community access and was having an impact on his further placements. The local athletics track had accessible cycling a couple of evenings a week, so Joey's personal assistant (PA) took him along and ran – they ran for the whole two-hour session, but they simply ran around and around the track. It was a managed risk, but was also a massive success. Joey and his very fit PA started running at other times; Joey absolutely loved the release that he got. Before every session, a very prescriptive set of 'laws' was read to Joey, with pictorial back-up. Sometimes things just seem to happen that can change lives – Joey's PA will have been very hard to replace!

Niall was a 12-year-old boy who would frequently strip off all of his clothing. This appeared to be random, with little or no pattern to the behaviour. Once stripped, Niall would become distressed and difficult. This behaviour appeared to meet several needs, including avoidance of certain activities – but not on every occasion. When he had to wait (on buses or taxis to go home or to go out), this could trigger this behaviour, but again not every time. There were occasions when there were queries about the 'feel' of certain clothes, but again it was not every time. When you cannot identify any trigger or obvious causation, putting in solutions can be difficult and problematic. A STAR (setting, trigger, action, response) analysis was undertaken over a number of weeks and it appeared that Niall's stripping did, in fact, meet several needs, depending on a number of factors. It became clear that there were inconsistencies from adults in responding to his behaviours. At times, it was evident that Niall's behaviour had an element of attention-seeking, and the way in which specific adults responded to Niall's inappropriate behaviours was inadvertently reinforcing the behaviour. It also appeared that he was sometimes very intolerant of specific items of clothing. This allowed discussion with parents, who were very supportive (Niall stripped at home and the parents also kept a detailed STAR analysis). Anxiety caused Niall to get hot and then his clothes became uncomfortable and off they came. Niall had anxiety around whether he was going to respite, as he would be on a different bus – one he didn't like. Another anxiety was around Niall's community access sessions. Niall received more information in an accessible format and this reduced some of his stress. Staff were supported in appropriate strategies to deal with the behaviour, maintaining Niall's dignity but, at the same time, not feeding his attention-seeking. The stripping reduced and Niall appeared more settled. His behaviours resurfaced periodically at times of major change – changing key stage or moving to adult services – and at these times it was a major concern to all involved. Thankfully, the episodes were short-lived, as there was a model in place to deal with it and this was shared with all staff to ensure consistent support.

Avoidance

Malik was attending a mainstream school, where he regularly avoided lessons by absconding from the classroom, often hiding in the PE storeroom. He was a capable pupil who created disruption for his peers and was failing to thrive in any area of the curriculum. Advice had been provided from the authority's ASD support team but the school found it difficult to be consistent in following the advice. Malik was referred to an ASD resource provision attached to a mainstream school, initially verbally abusing staff and rejecting learning opportunities. The consistent approach, high expectations of staff and calm ethos, underpinned by visual strategies making his day predictable, resulted in success, and before long Malik was engaging with peers in the mainstream classrooms. Looking at Malik with the benefit of hindsight and with an autism 'lens', his mainstream setting broke down due to the lack of consistency, which in turn created anxiety in Malik. Uncertainty in expectations had caused him to shut down; his flight, fight or freeze instinct took over. His placement at the ASD resource provision succeeded because they managed Malik's anxieties, creating an ethos that allowed him to achieve.

When Luther attended a mainstream school he struggled to cope, and soon learned that if he refused to work, disrupted the classroom, reacted rudely to the staff and damaged resources, his mum would be told to come and get him. When he was referred to a specialist ASD resource base, his daily routine had deteriorated to, at best, an hour in school before going home. Luther's mother was anxious about the change of school, as she did not have a car and would not be able to come to pick him up every morning when he misbehaved. She was assured that he would be in school all day, every day, and that the staff were confident in supporting him, managing his education and tailoring his curriculum to meet his needs. With visual support and calm, consistent interventions, affirming his strengths and supporting him with his difficulties, Luther settled in well, responded to his new environment and went from strength to strength.

Both Luther and Malik's reactions to mainstream education reflected the importance of considering the need for children with autism to receive accessible information about expectations – of behaviour and of outcomes – and to ensure consistency in application and the development of interventions that support success. When there is confusion or uncertainty, this will lead to anxiety, which may in turn result in difficult behaviours.

Avoidance behaviours are not uncommon; typically developing youngsters exhibit this type of behaviour – avoiding tidying the room or avoiding washing, for example! There is, however, a marked difference between a typical teenager avoiding a shower and the avoidance behaviour that may be expressed by a teenager with autism. Social anxiety may well have been the significant driver for both Luther and Malik; anxiety around social expectations and academic expectations made functioning in a socio-educational setting extremely problematic. The young man who had struggled through mainstream school in a very heightened level of arousal (which is exhausting in itself), who achieved good A level results at college and went on to university but could just not face any further unstructured social interaction and refused to leave his room for two years, was very different in his presentation of avoidance compared with any neurotypical, and this is OK.

Controlling behaviour

In many ways this is similar to avoidance – both are about the young person with autism desperately seeking an element of control and order in the neurotypical world. Many individuals on the spectrum have significant control challenges, and controlling behaviours can be one of the most challenging issues to contend with.

As mentioned previously, it is often difficult for individuals with autism to see the perspective of another. One reason why individuals with autism have difficulty coping is that they are lacking critical cognitive processing abilities, such as the theory of mind, which in turn renders daily life frustrating and often frightening. To make matters worse, there may be a lack of resilience. This, in turn, can result in wanting to make the rules, to enforce the rules and to take charge of others in an effort to keep things predictable and orderly. Harvey left a note for his teacher saying, 'If you would just do what I tell you, everything would be fine around here!' On the morning of the weekly community trip, he would arrive with an itinerary, planned route and instructions for the rest of the group. It was addressed by thanking him for his input and explaining that things were already organised. Issues also arose at home, as his mother explained when she rang to say that Harvey had put notes on the internal doors stating, 'Meeting tonight at 7.30 – be there.' She went on to say that they had all complied and his agenda was to tell each of them what they were doing wrong. Controlling the environment is the most effective means that these individuals like Harvey have to cope. The advice she was given was that if this occurred again, remove the notes, let Harvey know that the family got them and tell him that a family meeting would be convened when everyone was available. Regaining a sense of balance is very important.

Meltdowns or uncontrolled outbursts?

Many people on the autism spectrum will experience meltdowns. They can experience a complete loss of control, caused by being totally overwhelmed. Luther, Malik and Harvey were each attempting to control their environment in one way or another; sometimes the effort of coping in a hugely stimulating and stressful environment can be just too much and control is lost. **This is not a tantrum**.

The public can often find it hard to recognise a child with autism in severe distress. A child kicking, screaming, crying, swearing and throwing things in the supermarket may just have found it all too much. One actual event was when Jama had a major meltdown in a well-known supermarket as the clouds (meringue nests) had been moved because it was Christmas. It was the final straw; everything overwhelmed him and he just could not cope. The public can help by understanding autism, not judging and only offering help very subtly. We cannot pretend that differentiating is easy but erring on the side of understanding can be so helpful.

The management of behaviour that challenges can be difficult, and if not consistent in its delivery, it can exacerbate the situation. Prior to the 21st century, there was an emphasis on restraint to manage behaviour and staff were trained to do this appropriately to ensure the safety of everyone. Restraint or physical intervention was relatively common in school, day care and residential settings. Thankfully, the emphasis has changed for the better, and proactive, positive approaches are now the accepted interventions. By recognising the purpose of behaviour, remaining calm, diverting, distracting and understanding the individual and their specific needs, restraint is seldom necessary and should only ever be used as a last resort and only by those who are fully trained and qualified.

By looking very carefully and using all your detective skills to unravel the purpose of what you see, the young person can be better supported to reduce their anxiety without it resulting in loss of control, destruction, injury or distress. These skills must include your own demeanour, your body language, the volume of your voice and the calmness that you model. An angry face and a harsh voice create fear and raise anxiety rather than reducing it. This was the case with Alvis, when a teacher lost patience with him. He reached out at the person invading his space and grabbed her necklace, breaking the chain. This incident, provoked by an adult misinterpreting the situation, resulted in him being excluded from school. Could this have been prevented? Almost certainly, if the teacher had approached the situation with a calm, quiet voice and unthreatening posture.

Mindfulness

As we have seen, anxiety is frequently the driver in behaviour that challenges. Proactive approaches to the management of behaviour can include calming activities such as yoga, relaxation techniques and mindfulness. In one school, the entire student body gathered for assembly, where the interactive whiteboard showed the flames of a candle and a beautiful flower while everyone participated in the relaxation technique of 'smell the flowers' and 'blow out the candles'. The calmness was palpable.

Quiet spaces, planned-for exercise breaks, reducing demands, being sensitive to the hyper or hypo effects of sensitivities and maintaining a calm ethos all contribute to enabling children and young people to self-regulate and reduce the potential behaviours that challenge others. Most of us have ways to reduce tension, to self-calm when we become stressed. We recognise our own triggers and develop coping strategies to prevent us from 'going over the top'. For many individuals on the autism spectrum, the understanding and support of others to recognise triggers and learn to cope is essential.

Clarity and positive turn of phrase

It is so easy to respond to events negatively and inadvertently cause an escalation in these events. Clarity is very important. What does 'stop doing that' mean? Stop what? Don't do that. Don't do what? When an angry, confused child kicks his teacher, a raised voice and an angry face escalate the situation. Of course it hurts; of course you're not going to smile. But remaining calm, speaking quietly and giving a positive instruction can result in a totally different reaction. 'Feet down, it's OK.' The time to dissect the situation is **not** in the midst of it. Rather than 'stop hitting', instruct 'hands down' or 'hands in pockets'. Take time to reflect on how often you give a negative rather than a positive instruction and consider how this can be reversed. Liam was observed jumping very energetically during sessions, disrupting others and causing annoyance. His teacher responded with, 'Good jumping, Liam, now back to work' – simple, positive and effective.

Enabling the young person to recognise anger and supporting them in identifying coping strategies is essential. If the behaviour is 'owned' and self-control is internalised, the individual is given a tool for life. A good example of positive behaviour support was seen in a poster designed by a pupil. A self-portrait of an angry face was supplemented with coping strategies: 'When I feel angry, to help me calm down I can go somewhere quiet on my own, breathe deeply and slowly, hug a cushion or soft toy.' Presenting this visually and having it displayed for ready reference helped the strategies to be remembered by the pupil and enabled staff to offer gentle reminders.

Monica was struggling in a mainstream classroom and her mother was feeling worn down by the negative comments from her key worker. Every day the home–school communication book gave a litany of all of the things that Monica had done wrong. An advisory teacher was called in to observe her throughout the school day, provide support to staff and liaise with home. Throughout the observation, Monica was seen to cooperate and achieve the work that was set for her. She participated to the best of her ability until breaktime, when the group were invited to come to the front of the room to get their milk. Monica was caught up in the jostling, grabbing and chatter and could not cope. She rushed away and began to get upset. One other similar incident occurred during the day when the volume in the classroom was raised. If broken into time, 95 per cent of the day was positive. However, on a home visit, the home–school book was scrutinised and on that observation day, not one positive comment was made – the only feedback to Monica's mother was about the brief times when she was upset! Part of the advice to the school was to structure a new form of feedback, similar to this:

Date	Positive things today	Things to work on ☺

Change didn't occur overnight but gradually, with increased staff understanding and an emphasis on Monica's strengths, school became a positive experience for both Monica and her mother.

Anxiety and stress lead to loss of control. We can all admit that this has happened to us, with varying levels of anger. It can be so difficult to pull back from the situation, to let it go. When Leanne became upset, she would attempt to scratch those near her. She would sob and yell, 'Go away!' A successful strategy to calm the situation was for a different member of staff to swap with the person who was in her space. Through soothing words and a quiet and calm demeanour, the situation would frequently stop almost immediately. Helping young people to develop their own coping strategies is an effective and positive way forward. Mitchell had a short fuse and was particularly wound up by peers who commented on his work or appearance. He would strike out and physically scuffle with them. Debriefing after events, talking it through and looking at what else he could have done had a very positive effect on Mitchell. He began recognising when he was becoming upset, quietly asking to leave the room, putting some cold water on his face and taking some deep breaths. On returning, he would quietly tell staff, 'I'm OK now' and carry on. Not only did the incidents reduce because his provocateurs didn't get a rise from him, but his self-esteem was raised to new heights.

Emotional scales can be used to help a young person to recognise moods such as calm, restless, exhausted, anxious or ready to explode! The terms, of course, need to be understood. Accompanying these labels are descriptors of what happens at each phase and strategies of how to cope and return to calm. For example:

How am I feeling?	How do I know?	What can I do?
Restless	Fingers moving/ tapping Can't concentrate	Squeeze my stress ball Have a drink
Anxious	Want to hit Want to throw things	Go to a quiet place Take a break

Praise is not always responded to but for some individuals it is a useful tool. Appropriate rewards and use of special interests as motivators can be helpful in encouraging appropriate responses throughout the day. Abdi worked towards doing the laundry and helping the cleaning team – his reward was domesticity and watching the washing!

Sensitivity to the needs for a break, a spurt of exercise, a drink or a toilet break can encourage wellbeing and reduce the stress that leads to behaviour that is found challenging. Jane often dropped to the floor when walking, but through the use of 'first walk, then guitar', she would immediately get up and move forward. The guitar was a special interest, and brief times for enjoying it were built in during the day.

Anxiety is often linked to niggling worries. This was appropriately addressed in an assembly, where children role-played a story focused on worries as it was presented visually on the interactive whiteboard for all to see. In advance, peers from across the school had been asked to write down their worries and these had been attached to helium balloons. At the end of the assembly, the entire school went to the playground, where the balloons were released, with everyone waving goodbye to their worries.

Tip

The introduction to this book refers to the overlap of issues that individuals with autism often struggle with. When we fail to understand what we consider challenging behaviour, it is vital that we examine the complexities of communication, socialisation, resistance to change and sensory processing as contributing factors. Always consider the 'bigger picture' in searching for answers.

Challenging behaviour takeaways

- Be patient and realistic – behaviour very rarely changes overnight.
- Consistency is of paramount importance.
- Recognise the impact of the sensory environment.
- Effective and accessible communication is vital.

Behaviour

- Label emotions to promote understanding.
- Recognise the links between behaviour, communication and social issues.
- Reduce demands when signs of anxiety are evident.
- Manage change and transitions.
- Respect the individual.
- Always start afresh – do not carry incidents forward.
- Provide positive direction rather than negative reprimand.
- A supportive ethos and demeanour are essential.
- Discern when to intervene and when to stand back patiently.

6 The current climate

We write this book in strange times; the global pandemic has affected life in all aspects and we anticipate a new 'normal' without actually knowing what that will look like. We are not able to discuss what may happen in the field of autism, because there are still so many unknowns; however, this chapter will look at topics that remain relevant, regardless of the situation in which we find ourselves. We will be looking at:

- prevalence and some of the issues around getting accurate figures
- the journey to diagnosis for both children and adults
- autism awareness in the wider community
- educational provision – school and beyond
- employment
- adults with autism
- neurodiversity – is this the way forward?

Prevalence – the numbers game

In August 2013, an article in the *British Medical Journal* (Taylor et al.) stated that the 1990s had seen a fivefold increase in the numbers of children of school age diagnosed with an autism spectrum disorder. The number appeared to level off in the 2000s and since then there has been a steady increase in numbers. The UK's Parliament POSTnote of January 2020 states that 'Autism affects at least 1% of the population, although it is likely that this is underestimated, particularly in non-males.' This would mean that there are approximately 700,000 people with autism in the UK, and that 1.6 per cent of all school-age children in the UK may have autism. It is acknowledged that there is a very significant underrepresentation in these figures from adults, females, gender-fluid and non-binary and most Black, Asian and ethnic minority communities.

Underrepresentation in Black, Asian and ethnic minority communities

There is significant underrepresentation in Black, Asian and ethnic minority communities. This may be attributed to the following:

- There may be challenges in securing a diagnosis, due to lower levels of understanding of the condition in some communities and assumptions made by professionals, perhaps most notably when specific minority groups are labelled as having behaviour difficulties or pupils' communication difficulties are assumed to be as a result of English as a second language.

- Families reported to the National Autistic Society that they have found that schools and professionals are too quick to discount autism, assuming instead that problems are due to cultural, parenting or understanding issues.

- There may be cultural or language barriers in accessing services and there may be communication issues with professionals. Health, social and education providers need to be much more accessible to and engage with people from minority communities through improved communication. Professionals must be able to demonstrate greater cultural understanding and autism awareness. Services must be better placed to differentiate their responses to the specific autism needs of all communities. (National Autistic Society, 2014)

Sexuality, gender identity and autism

Gender identity and sexuality appear more varied in the autistic population compared to the general population. Autism is up to six times as common among people who are LGBTQI+ and some evidence suggests that autistic people are more likely to have gender dysphoria (National Autistic Society, undated). More research is required to understand the reasons behind this. One theory is that this prevalence may be linked to social norms. Typically, those labelled autistic are less influenced by social norms and therefore may be more comfortable to self-identify as gender diverse.

> 'A lot of us autistic people don't really fit in socially, and I think this extends to ideas around gender.'
>
> (Madge Woollard, autistic pianist, quoted in National Autistic Society, undated)

'The non-autistic world is governed by social and traditional expectations, but we may not notice these or fail to see them as important. This frees us up to connect more readily with our true gender.'
(Dr Wenn Lawson, autistic advocate, researcher and psychologist, quoted in National Autistic Society, undated)

Why do numbers matter?

In February 2020, the American Center for Disease Control (CDC) reported that approximately one in 54 children in the USA is diagnosed with an autism spectrum disorder, according to 2016 data (Autism Speaks, undated). The UK is unlikely to be significantly different from these numbers. The reality is that definitive numbers do not exist, as it is incredibly hard to quantify such a disparate group; autism is not a cohesive population – it very much is a 'spectrum'. However, there is little doubt that numbers are continuing to rise, although whether this is due to more precise diagnosis, more 'diluted' diagnostic criteria or a genuine rise in numbers is unclear.

There is an issue with not having a clear picture of numbers and that is that it makes it incredibly hard to predict the numbers needing services, the numbers of children who may need additional support and the numbers of adults who will require specialist services throughout their lives, for example. The economic impact of autism on individuals with the disorder, their families and society as a whole is poorly understood. It has been estimated that the cost over a lifetime would be in the region of £1.5 million for a person with autism with an additional learning difficulty. The cost of supporting children with autism in the UK has been estimated to be in the region of £2.7 billion per annum – a not insignificant sum.

What cannot be quantified is the emotional, psychological, financial and physical impact of autism – on individuals, on families and on the wider community.

The journey to a diagnosis

Many of those impacted by autism tell of a very long and difficult journey to diagnosis. Both adults and children can struggle to get clinicians to recognise the difficulties that they are experiencing. Currently, there is a range of tools that can be used to help the clinician come to a diagnosis: Autism Diagnostic Observation Schedule (ADOS), Diagnostic Interview for Social and Communication Disorders (DISCO) and Autism Diagnostic Interview – Revised (ADI-R), for example. Typically, the first port of call for parents would be either a health visitor or the family GP, who will then refer on to more specialist paediatric services. Often the concerns are raised either when milestones are missed or when there is a difference in social interaction at playgroup or nursery, for example.

If there is an obvious additional learning difficulty, an obvious difference in socialisation or significant behavioural difference, then an early diagnosis by a paediatrician is possible, leading to the possibility of early interventions. An early intervention with exposure to proven approaches such as 'Hanen' or 'EarlyBird' can help to ameliorate some of the differences, especially difficulties in communication or relationships. These interventions can be effective in supporting parents in their understanding of their child and their individual needs.

The end of key stages in school are significant points in a child's school life, and differences and difficulties are frequently highlighted. The school's SENDCo (special educational needs and disabilities coordinator) will perhaps raise concerns from class teachers – the move from Key Stage 1 to Key Stage 2 is a particular point where some additional needs are identified. If there are significant differences or difficulties, a referral may be made to an educational psychologist, who may, following assessment, refer on to CAMHS to secure a diagnosis. Getting a diagnosis at school age can allow additional support to be provided; however, a diagnosis does not necessarily mean that the child will need an EHCP (education health and care plan). Parents and/or school can ask for an EHC assessment ('statutory assessment') at any time. EHCPs can be an important tool that helps many children and young people with autism to access the additional support that they may need at school, at home or in the wider community.

EHCPs were introduced in the Children and Families Act 2014, replacing the 'statement of special educational needs'. They were intended to bring together education, social care and health services in one universal child-centred plan. EHCPs are for children and young people aged up to 25 who may need more support than is available through the school or college's internal additional support system. The EHCP is a legally binding document that identifies the 'special' needs of a child or young person and should also set out the kind of additional support that they will receive in school or in meeting their health and care needs. Not every child or young person with a diagnosis of autism will need or will receive an EHCP. There are a large number of organisations that can offer advice, support and guidance on the statutory assessment process, and it can be most beneficial to seek additional advice. See further information on page 157 for organisations to provide support and advice.

If there is no additional learning need or significant management issue, schools can be reluctant to support an EHC assessment, but the recognition of the mental health needs of young people is slowly improving and this may be the most appropriate pathway to securing a diagnosis and post-diagnostic support. The obstacle here can be the difficulty in accessing this pathway to CAMHS and the very limited availability of services; CAMHS are seriously overstretched and underfunded, and all too frequently it is a postcode lottery. However, given the importance of understanding the nature and impact of autism on an individual, timely intervention can significantly impact on your ability to deal with the implications.

The journey to diagnosis for adults can be even more challenging. There are adults who seek a diagnosis following on from the diagnosis of their child – a further pointer to the genetic nature of the condition, perhaps? There are some adults who seek a diagnosis after many decades of just feeling different. Asher had a good degree, had had several good jobs and could be described as fairly successful. However, he had two failed marriages, had attempted suicide at college and self-medicated his bouts of 'depression' through alcohol. His second wife had shouted, in one of their many arguments, that he was autistic – emotionally illiterate. At this point Asher sought help, and a very supportive GP helped him to access the adult mental health pathway, leading eventually to a diagnosis of Asperger syndrome. He said that lots of things made more sense to him; he read voraciously and researched it thoroughly. There is a happy ending here – Asher remarried his second wife, took early retirement and finally feels that he 'knows himself'. Getting such a diagnosis so late in life can be very difficult for some adults; suddenly you have a label, and this can be affirming or can be very difficult to come to terms with.

Over the last ten years there has been increasing recognition of the needs of adults with autism. The Autism Act (2009) laid down in statute the requirements to address these needs. More recently, NICE (National Institute for Health and Care Excellence) guidance was updated in 2016, outlining best practice in recognition, assessment and management for adults with autism. These guidelines should be read by any adult who is self-identifying as autistic, anyone who is supporting an autistic adult (in any way – as a spouse, for example) and those who are considering embarking on the diagnostic journey.

Like so much else, there is a postcode lottery in terms of accessing services for adults with autism, especially for those who have no additional learning disability. The services for adults have been decimated by ten years of austerity. The 2009 Autism Act placed a legal duty on all local authorities to develop a diagnostic pathway, and there is a cross-party agreement to revisit the act and update it. COVID-19 may have delayed further discussions, but lobbying groups will continue to push for action.

Why diagnosis can be so important

As we have seen, it can be hugely difficult to arrive at definitive numbers of those diagnosed as having autism in all its myriad of presentations. There are large sections of the community that are significantly underrepresented in any prevalence figures – those who are Black, Asian or minority ethnic and females in particular. There are significant numbers of adults who slip through the net, who 'manage' to function in society with autism but who don't have a diagnosis, don't want a diagnosis or may be unaware of the nature of their differences. However, the rise in adults seeking professional help with mental health difficulties has highlighted the hidden nature of autism in adulthood. Many people negotiate school and, perhaps, further or higher education very much on the periphery – perhaps not engaging in the social aspects or having a very small circle of friends. Many of the difficulties associated with an autism spectrum condition can be masked or hidden successfully. These difficulties may not impact on an individual until they hit a certain level in employment – managing staff, for example, or face-to-face meetings with clients – or until they are in a 'serious' relationship.

Diagnosis in adulthood can be problematic, with reports of GPs simply not recognising it or taking the issues seriously, and accessing the adult diagnostic pathways remains a challenge in many areas. However, securing the diagnosis can give meaning to the difficulties that the adult has encountered; the issues can be addressed and the 'differences' make some sense to the individual. An increasing number of women have written accounts of receiving the diagnosis of autism in adulthood and the impact that it has had on their lives (BBC Radio 4, 2020, 'Broad spectrum').

At school age it should be easier to identify whether an individual is having some difficulties, either socially or academically – it should be, but it isn't always, straightforward. We have seen in previous chapters how young people will present very differently in different settings. Children who have 'kept it together' for the six hours at school come home and there is often a huge release of pent-up anxiety, emotion and stress. Parents then experience the 'after-school restraint collapse': the child has a safe place to let it all out – tears, aggression; it can take on many presentations – but the key thing is that it is hidden from schools. The school will not recognise the difficulties because the child masks, hides or suppresses all the anxieties and stresses that they may experience at school. Many parents report that unless there is a classroom management issue or an obvious additional learning need, many schools simply do not support the diagnostic search. The Child and Family Act 2014 and the changes to the whole SEND process do not seem to have improved the situation, and parents continue to encounter significant battles to get the differences recognised, identified and hence assessed for a potential diagnosis.

Diagnosis can make some sense of the differences and difficulties that the child encounters. It can also reduce the family's feelings of failure; as one parent expressed, 'If you had a rash, you would want to know the cause – you might not be able to do much about it, but at least you know where it has come from.' A diagnosis can be a signpost – you may not want to take that road, but at least you know the direction!

Where are all the girls?

Statistically there are considerably more boys with autism. This skewing of the ratio between the sexes has been recognised since Kanner and Asperger first defined the disorder. The reasons behind this are perhaps more contentious. It could be rooted in biological differences between the sexes. Or, perhaps, it may be the result of the way in which autism has been defined and diagnosed.

A study of autism's sex ratio, published in 2017 in the *American Journal of Child and Adolescent Psychiatry* (Loomes et al., 2017), examined data from prevalence studies worldwide. That analysis estimated about 4.2 boys with autism for every girl; however, further analysis of the data suggested that a more appropriate ratio may be closer to 3:1. Girls with autism appear to be missed because diagnosticians too often think of autism as primarily affecting boys, and typically girls may also be better than boys at masking the symptoms of autism. Either way, autism is probably significantly underdiagnosed in girls. Typically, girls receive a diagnosis later than boys, backing up the hypothesis that girls can mask many of the subtle symptoms that are more overtly presented in boys – boys often have special interests such as *Thomas the Tank Engine*, leading to trainspotting, as opposed to girls, who do appear to have fewer special interests, and those interests may fit better into the expected norm. Autism looks different in girls and perhaps it is this that results in late diagnosis.

It is unlikely, even with more precise diagnosis and identification, that the gender ratio would come down below 3:1 even when actively looking, based on the biological differences between boys and girls – there are differences in the structures within the brains of males and females.

Male and female differences?

Autism diagnostic characteristics have largely been based on the male presentations, and therefore the diagnostic assessments of core autistic symptoms show considerably poorer sensitivity towards females than males, resulting in missed or delayed identification and reduced availability of support services for females with autism.

Research is just beginning to turn the appropriate amount of attention to autism characteristics in girls and women. Emerging research shows that autism-related behaviours are qualitatively different in females. Further, girls and women tend to present with more camouflaging behaviours, which have been linked to higher rates of significant mental health difficulties. Research into the neurobiological underpinnings of such sex differences is still in its early days. Understanding the brain-basis of sex differences in autism is paramount for the eventual accurate diagnosis of females and for providing sex-specific interventions.

One issue that does need addressing if we are to get a more balanced view of the ratio between boys and girls is the actual diagnostic process and the manual that is typically used – most screening and diagnostic tools are based largely on observations of behaviours in males. As a result, we may still be missing girls whose symptoms do not match the 'prototypical' boy presentation. Even if a girl has subtler difficulties than other children with the disorder, those problems may nevertheless have a profound impact on her life.

> 'We are different from the boys.'
> (Limpsfield Grange School for girls with autism spectrum conditions, cited in 'Girls and autism: Flying under the radar' by NASEN, 2016)

Some ideas to help girls with autism:

- Try to build girls' own age-appropriate understanding of autism, sensory sensitivities and anxieties, and how to manage them.
- Use social language programmes to navigate social rules, with peer-mentoring schemes for friendship and bullying issues.
- Use personal, social and health education specifically to facilitate:
  - sex and relationship education – adolescence is unpredictable
  - bodily changes
  - heightened anxiety due to perceived lack of control
  - independence, to reduce vulnerability
  - privacy awareness, personal space and touching rules
  - permission to say 'No'
  - awareness of e-safety and grooming – girls with autism spectrum conditions are more vulnerable to complying with a demand and are more likely to respond to communication.
- If girls 'mirror', carefully select appropriate peers to model responses.

- If girls are socially immature and vulnerable, provide more structured activities during social times.
- Girls can try to impose controlling play on their peers, so model reciprocity.

Autism awareness in the wider community

Dustin Hoffman playing an adult with autism was perhaps the first acknowledged portrayal of autism in the popular media. It was, without doubt, a double-edged sword. People's understanding and awareness of the condition certainly increased exponentially. The issue was that the character of Raymond in *Rain Man* became synonymous with autism; everyone who had autism was a mathematical genius with an amazing memory – not quite the reality!

In 2020, we have now had characters with autism in *Grange Hill*, *EastEnders*, *Sesame Street* and many more mainstream programmes. CBeebies has a programme where the main character has autism. *The A Word*, a BBC TV drama, has shown, warts and all, many of the issues with raising a child with autism. Adults with autism have been very well portrayed in dramas such as *Casualty*, *The Good Doctor* and *Bones*. The best-selling novel *The Curious Incident of the Dog in the Night-Time* has been successfully adapted as a stage play, and the book and play both give a remarkable insight into the world of autism. These are all very significant steps in the recognition and acceptance of the condition across the wider community.

Many supermarkets and shopping centres have monthly 'autism-friendly' quiet sessions, as do cinemas – they turn down the volume a notch, often have the lights on and 'allow' the viewers to wander around. There are Premier League football grounds with sensory rooms and other autism-friendly adaptations. The inclusion agenda is making a difference – small steps but, nonetheless, progress is being made.

Airports, hospitals and civic buildings are being 'labelled' as autism-friendly, with staff who have received autism training. From experience, this is working – a visit to the children's A&E department with a pupil who had had a nasty fall would previously have been an experience that would have been particularly challenging. However, this department has nurses who are autism champions; they have had more than mandatory training and there are adaptations made within the department's protocols and practices. The pupil did not have to experience the long wait; the triage system was bypassed and the staff used PECS® and a tablet with a communication system on it – all recognisable and reassuring for the pupil. The whole visit was not the traumatic and difficult experience that it so frequently used to be (and can continue to be for a great many people on the spectrum).

Autism Champions or ambassadors are making a real difference for individuals and families in wider society.

Autism Champions (or ambassadors)

Many organisations – hospitals, Manchester Airport and the Trafford Centre, for example – have identified individuals (or several individuals) who strive to ensure that their company, facility or organisation becomes as autism-friendly as possible. In many cases, the individuals have a good understanding, acceptance and knowledge of autism that they can share within their organisation, business, department or team. Most likely they will have completed an appropriate level of training about autism and be able to offer support and pass on the knowledge that they have learned to the rest of the staff they work with. An Autism Champion will be able to develop local expertise through their knowledge and understanding and improve practice in supporting autistic people and their families to access services.

The criminal justice system

Research from the University of Salford (Hepworth, 2017) suggests that individuals with autism are up to seven times more likely to enter the criminal justice system (CJS) than their neurotypical peers. Many common 'symptoms' of autism, such as poor communication and interpersonal skills, may be interpreted as incriminating, putting those with autism at a disadvantage from the very beginning of contact with the wider CJS. Police will often be very suspicious of someone who does not speak, who doesn't make eye contact or who is seen as acting strangely. The weekly visit to the local butcher's shop became a traumatic experience for one young man with autism. The aromas within meant that Rhys waited outside for his dad, standing where he could be seen through the large shop window. This regular routine had proven to be positive for months. On this Saturday, when Rhys's dad looked up from the counter, he saw two police officers with his son. Rhys had been waving his arms and making loud utterances that drew the attention of a passer-by. Being concerned, she alerted the police. As they approached Rhys he became anxious and continued to swing his arms in their direction; being non-verbal, he was unable to answer their questions and, as they persisted, he became more frightened. His heightened anxiety and fear led to them handcuffing him. As Rhys's father emerged from the shop, his son was in a terrible state of panic, and although his dad was able to explain the situation and 'rescue' his son, the experience had a profound impact on Rhys and his family. The officers involved had been unprepared for the reaction that their approach invoked, and had no understanding of the heightened anxiety of an individual with complex autism. Hopefully, they learned a lesson that day; hopefully, in a similar situation they would act differently, stand back, allow space, speak quietly and assess whether a family member or support worker was nearby. We can hope that they shared their experience with colleagues as a way to learn from their own experiences. Lack of training and understanding can and does exacerbate situations that arise in public settings, and as awareness grows in society, such incidences, hopefully, will reduce.

As we have just learned, the behaviours of a person with autism can make an individual more vulnerable to aspects of the CJS, and may also increase their risk of becoming involved with the police or CJS in the first instance. Lobbying groups, autism charities and other organisations have been working hard with police forces across the country to improve understanding and awareness. The National Autistic Society has accredited Her Majesty's Young Offenders Institute (HMYOI) Feltham for their practice, procedures and policies in dealing with young offenders on the spectrum. A private member's bill was brought before Parliament to ensure that all police forces were required to train their officers in autism. The bill failed; however, it has been promised to come before the Commons again and has kept the issue very much in the spotlight. Autism alert cards are also being used in a number of police forces; the National Police Autism Association has been prominent in developing 'alert cards', promoting the development of Autism Champions in police forces across the country. You can download the alert card for the West Midlands, for example, at this link: https://autismwestmidlands.org.uk/home/alert-cards.

Small steps are being taken by public bodies in improving the lived experience for people on the spectrum – there is still a huge amount to do, but the last ten years have seen a sea of change in attitudes.

- Get to know your local authority's 'Local Offer' inside out; it should provide a comprehensive list of services and support for people with additional needs.
- The National Autistic Society and local autism support groups frequently provide an 'alert' card – it can be very useful to hand out at those times when the public are just not getting it!
- Many major airports make allowances for families living with autism, such as access to a room, priority boarding or escorting through security.
- If you do not ask, you will not get!

The Autism Act 2009

The Act attempted to achieve two things: the government must prepare and regularly review a national strategy for the provision of services for adults with autism, and the government was required to produce statutory guidance for all local authorities on the implementation of the strategy at a local level.

The Act has had some positive impact across the country, with the vast majority of local authorities now having an adult diagnostic pathway, and a substantial number of local authorities having a named officer who is responsible for the autism strategy. However, an inquiry into the impact of the Autism Act ten years after its introduction, published by the All Party Parliamentary Group on Autism (APPGA) and the National Autistic Society, found that there is simply not enough care, support and understanding in society for autistic people in England. Two in three autistic adults are not getting the support that they need, meaning that up to 327,000 autistic adults are not getting help to do things that we can take for granted, such as socialising, sustaining employment, managing money or getting out and about.

The past ten years of 'austerity' have had a massive impact on the provision of local authority services across the country, and autism services have been impacted by the cuts and the rationalisation in adult social care provision: only five per cent of adults with autism now get the support that they need to live more independently, and befriending or buddying is only available to four per cent of those who would benefit from this support (APPGA and National Autistic Society, 2019). This is having devastating consequences for autistic people: widespread isolation, mental health problems and people falling into crisis.

While the current situation is 'not enough', the achievements of the Autism Act are significant and it remains the only parliamentary legislation dedicated to improving support and services for a specific disability. The continued lobbying by charities and parents will hopefully ensure that the new autism strategy, which is pledged to include provision for children, actually brings the changes that are so needed.

Educational provision

Schools are potentially well placed to have a positive impact on the lives of those with autism and their families. Where schools are most successful in dealing with autism, they have an ethos that understands the complexity of those pupils with additional needs in all their forms (including autism) – an ethos that is inclusive, accepting and supportive, enabling all youngsters to achieve. There are many examples of young people with significant difficulties with their autism in the early years who, given the correct interventions and support, are enabled to go on to achieve degrees or success in business or industry, and who have achieved their full potential. There are some real success stories out there, from Temple Grandin to Susan Boyle to Chris Packham and many more in between. There are examples of adults with very complex autism who have celebrated talents in areas such as visual art or music, and yet they continue to need significant support in their daily lives. For many others, their success is evident through greater independence – small steps of self-help skills and internalising strategies that reduce anxiety.

That said, success stories are not always experienced by families and individuals.

> - 'Exclusions for children with autism have risen sharply – up by almost 60% across England – in five years.
> - In every English region, exclusions of children with autism have increased by at least 44%.
> - In contrast overall exclusions have risen by 4% in the same period.'
>
> (Ambitious about Autism, 2018, 'We need an education' report)

The 2014 Children and Families Act (CAF) intended to bring about some significant changes for all children with SEND. The new code of practice and the statutory duties that it included, the new assessment of need and the school responsibilities were all supposed to be game-changers – certainly, the very laudable aim of getting education, health and social care to work together could have made a big impact.

Key aspects of the 2014 SEND legislation (Department for Education) were:

- Ensure that young people and their parents have the information they need about their disability or special educational needs.

- Ensure that children, young people and families know what help they can get when a child or young person has special educational needs or a disability.

- Ensure that different organisations work together to help children and young people with special educational needs.

- Give children and young people and their parents more say about the help that they may get.

- Set up one assessment to look at what special help a child or young person needs with their education, as well as their health and social care needs, all at the same time.

- Give a child or young person just one plan for meeting their education, health and social care needs, which can run from birth to age 25 if councils agree that a young person needs more time to get ready for adulthood.
- Ensure that children, young people and their parents can choose some of the help that they need.
- Provide ways to help sort things out if a child or young person or their parent needs to appeal about the help they get.

With all the good intentions enshrined in the CAF 2014, why are exclusions continuing to rise? Why do so many children with autism have such a torrid time at school? Why is the education system letting so many down?

School is one of the most challenging environments for children on the autism spectrum, because of the social demands and potential for sensory overload, as well as the academic pressure. Our 'round hole' education system is not wonderfully accommodating for children who can appear to be a square peg. Autistic children and young people are too frequently seen as management problems, and schools do not always recognise their strengths and individual talents. Mainstream schools in particular have been struggling to successfully accommodate and work with pupils with autism.

Given the diversity within the spectrum and between individuals, there is no single educational intervention that is useful for all children on the autism spectrum, and there is no single intervention that would on its own be sufficient to meet all the needs of a particular child on the autism spectrum. Education needs to be individualised, to allow for different needs and for different teaching goals at different times. In all the comparative evaluations of educational interventions, it is always the case that some children respond well to a specific intervention and others do not. Unlike most neurotypical children, who learn to apply and use skills and knowledge across situations and contexts and can pick up skills incidentally, children with autism will frequently need to be taught skills explicitly and then taught to use these across situations.

There are schools and settings that are successful, however, and they generally take on board elements of proven interventions. If you were to visit autism-specific schools, you would see some commonality and some significant similarities across these settings.

The SPELL approach underpins many of the most effective schools. SPELL is the National Autistic Society's framework for understanding and responding to the needs of autistic children and adults.

- **Structure:** This makes the world a more predictable, accessible and safer place. By creating structured environments using visual information, pupils are supported, developing independence and reducing dependence on others. Environments and processes can be modified to ensure that each person knows what is going to happen and what is expected of them, thereby reducing anxiety.

- **Positive (approaches and expectations):** Schools and services establish and reinforce self-confidence and self-esteem by building on natural strengths, interests and abilities. Expectations of children and students should be high but realistic and based on thorough assessment. Assessments should be taken from a range of perspectives and should include noting the barriers to accessing opportunity.

- **Empathy:** We neurotypicals should try to see the world through the eyes of an autistic child or adult, knowing what it is that motivates or interests them but also, importantly, what may frighten, preoccupy or otherwise distress them. Making efforts to understand, respect and relate to the experience of the autistic person must underpin a successful setting's attempt to develop communication and reduce anxiety. The quality of the relationship between the person with autism and their 'supporters' is vitally important. Effective supporters are calm, predictable, good-humoured, empathetic and analytical.

- **Low arousal:** Approaches and the environment should be calm and ordered in such a way as to reduce anxiety and aid concentration. There should be as few distractions as possible, paying attention to noise levels, colour schemes, odours, lighting and clutter, for example. Some people may need more time to process information, especially speech. Clear information should be given in the medium best suited to the individual, with care taken not to overload or bombard.

- **Links:** Autistic people and their parents or advocates should be seen as partners. Schools should recognise the benefits of sharing information and working alongside the individual, their families and other professionals. Open links and communication will reduce the risk of misunderstanding, confusion or the adoption of fragmented, piecemeal approaches. Schools should create and maintain links between the individual, their wider support networks and the community.

TEACCH (Treatment and Education of Autistic and Communication Handicapped Children) is a whole-life system developed in North Carolina in the 1960s. TEACCH is a structured methodology that focuses on the individual and their need for familiarity and predictability; it addresses the receptive communication difficulties and promotes understanding. Effective autism-specific schools and services may well have a strong underpinning of the TEACCH values: **t**eaching and learning about autism and the culture of autism; **e**xpanding individual skills, knowledge and abilities and expanding community knowledge and understanding of autism; **a**ppreciating the individual's strengths and abilities; **c**ollaboration and **c**ooperation with the wider community and the autistic community in particular; and **h**olistic working with the community impacted by autism – a whole-community approach is needed to make a lasting difference.

As we have seen in previous chapters, there are many examples of schools, both mainstream and special, who adapt these principles (both SPELL and TEACCH) to meet their pupils' needs. These interventions are often able to support successes within the school. Successful schools are inclusive, aspirational and able to meet the needs of an increasingly complex and diverse population; they do exist, they might just need a bit of searching out.

> **Fewer than half of children with autism are happy at school, seven out of ten felt that their classmates did not understand them and 50 per cent felt that their teachers didn't know how to support them or meet their educational needs.**
>
> (Ambitious about Autism, 2018, 'We need an education' report)

Further and higher education

With the current prevalence figures, every college and university will have students (and staff) who have autism. Like so much else in the 'autism world', the success of any placement is predicated on preparation, good planning and careful thought. Many autistic students achieve degrees and have fruitful and successful experiences in further or higher education. All colleges and universities have members of staff who have a responsibility for students with additional needs. Many establishments will offer learning mentors and personal tutors who will have good knowledge of the issues that will undoubtedly arise. Steve was a student who started his school career in a specialist autism provision; he transferred at Key Stage 3 to a supportive (but very large) Catholic comprehensive school. He achieved a number of good GCSE passes and moved on to a tertiary college for A levels. When Steve moved on to a 'campus' university in north-west England, things looked very promising. However, the reality was somewhat different. Steve found the lack of structure extremely challenging, he found the social aspect of university life very difficult and 20 years ago universities were not very accommodating or particularly flexible. Steve's mum fought hard to get the university to take their responsibilities seriously in terms of the Disability Discrimination Act. Steve got a named mentor, a personal tutor with personal experience of the condition, and he achieved a really good degree (2:1!). The university learned very quickly and developed its 'offer' to students on the spectrum; it also achieved 'autism friendly status' across the campus and on individual courses.

The National Autistic Society provides a good range of advice and guidance for students – and those supporting them – looking to go on to university. It should be remembered that all colleges and universities have a legal duty under the Equality Act (2010) to make 'all' reasonable adjustments to ensure that no student with a disability (and that definition includes autism) should be put at a substantial disadvantage, including in relation to both educational and social opportunities. These reasonable adjustments for autistic students can include, for example, an individualised transition and induction programme, additional settling-in time and a named member of staff to approach if there are worries or concerns (in the best cases this is a two-way process). The establishment should have received autism-awareness training and provide alternative learning pathways, including adapted course materials. Many establishments will now signpost students to more appropriate accommodation; large student halls or digs are not always the most autism-friendly.

Potential students should check what reasonable adjustments and access arrangements can be made for them with the disability services team at the college or university as soon as possible. The students' union will often have an elected student representative as a welfare or disability officer who can be a point of contact and support regarding the social aspects of university or college life.

Autism should not be a barrier to a successful university or college experience.

Adults with autism

As mentioned previously, approximately one in 100 adults are autistic (UK Parliament, 2020) and, matching the profile of children with autism, there is a huge variation in the presentation of the disorder in these individuals. However, these numbers warrant a closer examination. The one in 100 figure is in fact 13 years old and was arrived at by NHS England by simply following the numbers of children with a diagnosis. This statistic is based on a study that focused entirely on adults with learning disabilities, which will not include all autistic people, as not all autistic people have a 'learning disability' (around 50 per cent of autistic people have no learning disability at all). We can see that the numbers are conflicting and often not based on secure foundations. Achieving more precise numbers is important in developing services and predicating the need for services in the future. For a variety of reasons, adults with autism often struggle to access the help and support that they need and want. This has a significant impact on their lives, their independence and their families and can lead to social isolation. Securing the appropriate support can allow the autistic population to reach their potential and, whenever possible, gain employment.

The Autism Act put a statutory responsibility on the government to produce a national strategy that intended to give clear guidance to all local authorities and health authorities. A number of other statutory duties are also included in the Care Act (2014), the Equality Act (2010), the Mental Capacity Act (2005) and the Mental Health Act (2007, updated in 2017). These acts specifically identify the responsibilities of local authorities and or health authorities, including diagnosis and assessment of need. The autistic adult population with a difficulty in learning or additional needs is served with varying degrees of success by local social care providers, and the provision of autism-specific adult services is increasing both in numbers and in efficacy. There are outstanding examples of services where appropriate employment and worthwhile and meaningful day services are being provided; unfortunately, there remains a degree of postcode lottery in accessing these services. There are also numerous very negative press reports that highlight significant issues with the care of adults with autism and learning difficulties in a wide range of settings, and these must add to the anxieties of parents already worrying about the future for their sons or daughters.

The adults with autism who do not have additional learning needs very frequently fall through the gaps in accessing support, even though they would hugely benefit from these services. To access any services, eligibility has to be met; unfortunately, the assessment process has become politicised over the past ten years. To meet the criteria, you currently need to demonstrate that:

1. Your needs for care and support arise from specific health problems.

2. As a result, you're unable to do certain things.

3. There is a significant impact on your wellbeing.

Autism per se does not meet the criteria; you have to demonstrate that your autism impacts on your mental health, has an impact on learning or cognitive abilities, or causes you ill health. Demonstrating the impact of your autism can be a challenge, and there are not always appropriate support services available to meet very specific needs.

Employment

Only 16 per cent of adults with autism are in paid employment. In contrast, 80 per cent of the neurotypical working-age population are in employment of one sort or another and, looking at the wider 'disabled' population, 47 per cent are in some sort of employment (National Autistic Society, 2016). That figure for the autistic population is extremely low and reflects the difficulties that adults with autism encounter. There is also a financial impact to consider. The cost of supporting children with autism was estimated in 2009 to be in the region of £2.7 billion per annum; the cost of supporting adults was £25 billion per annum (Knapp et al., 2009) – a significant amount. Clearly not all adults with autism are able to be in 'employed' work; however, with understanding employers and reasonable adjustment being made, many autistic people have the potential to be real assets to businesses. Support of one kind or another has been identified as the intervention that could have the biggest impact on success in the workplace for people with autism. Workplace support can take many forms: it could be a mentor (a named colleague who can address issues for and with the autistic person) or it may be that the business provides a room so that the person with autism can de-stress. Consideration should be given to the physical environment, personal space and proximity.

Any workplace has a significant social aspect and it can be in this area that most difficulties are encountered – the unwritten rules of the office and the typical office 'banter' have the potential to lead to stress and anxiety. Reasonable adjustments in a workplace could take the form of clearly written guidelines, expectations and instructions in clear, unambiguous language. It is important to carefully consider the disclosure of the diagnosis; this would allow work colleagues to have a greater understanding of the nature of the difficulties and could allow autism and diversity training to be provided – and in actual fact there should be no need to hide a diagnosis of autism.

An employee with autism has the potential to offer their employer a variety of sometimes exceptional skills that enable them to thrive in roles ranging from sales assistant to computer programmer, and journalist to statistician. As well as their individual strengths and talents, autistic employees can often demonstrate above-average skills in some or all of the following areas:

- high levels of concentration and focus
- reliability, conscientiousness and persistence
- accuracy, close attention to detail and the ability to identify errors

- technical ability, such as in IT
- detailed factual knowledge and an excellent memory.

This means that an autistic person may well be better at a particular job than someone who is not autistic. By gaining an understanding of autism, any employer can open up new possibilities, and indeed companies such as Microsoft, Google, UBS and Barclays actively recruit people with autism for the attributes identified above. Employing autistic people demonstrates that the organisation has a commitment to equality and diversity and shows a positive attitude towards disabled people.

Neurodiversity

There is a growing movement within the autism community that thinks not in terms of 'curing' a disorder but instead about celebrating diversity. Autism is seen as a difference, a neurological difference to be recognised and respected like any other human difference and variation. As such, neurodiversity activists reject the idea that autism should be cured, advocating instead for celebrating autistic forms of communication and self-expression, and for promoting support systems that allow autistic people to live as autistic people. This is not to suggest that autistic people do not find everyday life a challenge, but instead that they see it as a different way of communicating, thinking and interacting. These differences should be respected.

Pathological demand avoidance (PDA)

PDA is a relatively new term for an autistic presentation that is identified by an extreme avoidance of everyday expectations and demands, most frequently accompanied by extreme anxiety. As yet, it is not a universally accepted diagnosis. Typically, those described as PDA appear to have more developed social understanding and communication skills than some other autistic people, and will appear to use this to their advantage. However, this apparent sociability will frequently mask difficulty with processing and understanding communication and social situations. Children and young people with this profile often appear as excessively controlling and dominating, especially when feeling anxious (in school, for example). If the young person can be given a feeling of control and security, then they are more confident and engaging and can achieve. Regardless, it's important to acknowledge that these young people have a significant hidden difference that can be extremely disabling. When supporting a young person with a PDA profile, it's important to recognise that they are not deliberately choosing to be oppositional or defiant – they are having difficulty adapting and overcoming their need to be in control of their environment, and are likely to be extremely anxious. Giving the correct support and interventions may therefore mean that their trust and self-confidence grows, and with it their ability to cope more flexibly with the everyday demands of life. PDA pupils and students need a different approach in schools; the familiar and proven methodologies for other autistic pupils are not always effective.

Too often, PDA is seen as a deliberate choice that the young person is making; this links them into the 'social, emotional and mental health' category in statutory assessment. PDA is not the same as oppositional defiant disorder and not recognising the fundamental difference between the two does a disservice to the young people who are so significantly 'disabled' by their anxieties.

Mental health implications

Those with autism in all its presentations are at higher risk of mental health issues than the neurotypical population. This may be because there are fewer resources and support for people with autism to help them to develop coping skills, and they frequently experience more negative life events. People with autism all too frequently face stigma and discrimination from people and services as a result of their disability. Biology and genetics may also have a significant impact on the increase in the likelihood of developing a mental health problem.

However, the mental health of people with autism or a learning disability (or both) is often overlooked or ignored. Up to eight out of ten people with autism will have some additional mental health issues such as OCD (obsessive compulsive disorder), bipolar disorder, depression or an anxiety disorder. A communication difference such as autism can make talking about depression and anxiety extremely problematic, and too often mental health problems are just seen as part of autism.

> ### Tip
>
> The key is in the recognition of the problem. Seeking professional help and advice is essential and often needs those supporting the individual to advocate for them and to help clarify the issues or concerns.

Causation and cure?

Are we any closer to identifying the real cause of autism? The truth is that it appears to be a multifactorial issue – there are many genes that have been linked but no single genetic cause has been identified. A number of physical factors have been linked to brain development; however, it is not a result of emotional deprivation or a result of parenting.

Although there has been significant news coverage about MMR and autism, there is absolutely no evidence to link autism with vaccines of any sort – full stop, period!

Autism is a spectrum condition and therefore it should be expected that there may be a spectrum of causes; while there may be a common diagnostic term and a degree of commonality in symptoms, there is a myriad of presentations of the condition.

There is no cure, as it is a lifelong condition. Autism is a difference and not a disadvantage; it needs to be accepted, understood and embraced. Each person with autism faces challenges and difficulties; however, there are strengths, abilities and talents that cannot be overlooked.

> 'If you got rid of all the autism genetics, you wouldn't have science or art. All you would have is a bunch of social "yak yaks".'
>
> (Temple Grandin, quoted in Raymond, 2010)

Where next?

Could autism be increasing because it is the next stage of the human evolutionary journey? Perhaps – as we become more and more dependent on computers and less on social interaction – it's not too far-fetched. Certainly, Temple Grandin feels so! Regardless, it is clear that the incidence of autism is increasing, and it is unlikely to be down to simple improvements in the diagnostic process nor the dilution of the diagnosis; there is a small statistically significant rise in numbers. This has serious implications for strategic planning and the development of services, for schools, adult services and social care, and for the NHS and CAMHS. We as a society need to listen carefully to the autism community and work together to develop interventions, services and provisions that truly meet the needs of all people who are diagnosed on the autism spectrum.

Current climate takeaways

- There is no cure for autism – it is a lifelong, pervasive *difference* and should be seen as such.
- The pathway to a diagnosis, both for adults and for children, can often be long and challenging; a diagnosis is both a signpost and a key to open doors.
- There is considerable work to be done to ensure that those with autism are able to work and be supported to maintain that employment – autism is very significantly underrepresented in the workplace.
- People with autism are significantly overrepresented in mental health services and in negative experiences with both police and the CJS.
- Children with autism too frequently still have negative experiences in all aspects of education.
- The Autism Act had the potential to be a groundbreaking piece of legislation – it is not too late to make it so.
- The positive aspects of the diagnosis are beginning to be recognised in the technology, computing and banking industries – barriers are slowly being removed.
- Autism awareness, recognition and acceptance is increasing, which can only be a good thing.
- There are many undiagnosed individuals on the spectrum who are coping and making a significant contribution in the workplace.

7 Impact on families: The highs and lows

Every family is unique and responds to the diagnosis and needs of their child or children with autism in their own way. At times there are expressions of frustration and despair while at others there are celebrations and triumphs. The commitment, determination, love and acceptance of families is often beyond measure. Looking at the issues realistically and celebrating the successes will be addressed in this chapter, including:

- the journey of parenting
- difficult choices
- positive experiences
- needs of siblings
- transitions
- future concerns
- aspirations.

The challenges of parenting

Every parent faces challenges in their daily responsibility to nurture and support the development of their children. This is indeed a 24/7 commitment that carries on into adulthood.

The previous chapter outlines many of the reasons why these challenges are magnified when parenting a child on the autism spectrum. Things that are often taken for granted become stumbling blocks. Systems that work for *most* seem to be landmines when negotiating the journey of understanding assessment, diagnosis and support within the world of autism.

Parents often express this central goal: to love, accept and respect them as a person, and for them to be included as a member of the family and understood and embraced by society. Many are devoted to helping their child be the best that they can be and give their lives to this pursuit. One family described their son with autism as the catalyst that drew the family closer, creating an unbreakable bond as they worked together to help him experience every opportunity to enrich his life.

The disappointments

For some parents, coming to terms with a diagnosis of autism is a relief – finally understanding why their child is developing in a different way than expected and enabling them to find strategies to intervene. Other families receive the information with a sense of disbelief, rejection and despair. We have worked with parents who grieved for the future with heartfelt questions such as, 'Will she ever be able to kick a ball with me?' and 'Will he ever get married and have a life of his own?' It takes time to accept, adjust, develop understanding and move forward.

Some parents worry about a stigma and try to hide the diagnosis, fearing that others will reject the child or the family. How can this be in the 21st century, when we are so familiar and, supposedly, committed to making progress with diversity, disability and inclusion?

For families where the extended family embraces and supports the individual with autism, they are blessed. The opportunities for respite with aunts and uncles and grandparents, the shared meals, the support for appointments and child-minding are all so very positive. Sadly, some families feel abandoned by everyone and have no support, no listening ears and no shoulders to cry on when things are difficult.

Listening to parents' disappointment when they realise that their child is excluded from peers' birthday parties, finds it difficult to make friends and is reprimanded for failing to follow the unwritten social rules is too common. These situations lead to real pain and often cause the family to withdraw and face social isolation.

The frustrations

Many parents feel as if their world has fallen through when they receive a diagnosis. Even though they may have recognised that development was not as expected, the assessment process and outcomes can be frightening. For others, they were oblivious to any concerns and the health visitor, nursery manager or school expressed concerns and recommended assessment. There are many paths that lead to the search for answers and eventual outcome. And then the journey begins!

One frequent frustration is the follow-up after the confirmation of a diagnosis of autism. Too often there is little support offered, with many parents reporting that they are given the contact details for the National Autistic Society and no personal, local or humanly accessible support. One parent wept as she said that they went home totally confused, cried all night, foresaw a dismal future for their four-year-old son and struggled to find the strength to look for answers. **This is just not good enough!**

For many years, campaigners have been advocating for a menu of provision to meet the unique needs of children and young people with autism. One principle in education is that a child should receive education in 'the least restrictive' setting. What this means in reality is often very confusing. It has too often led to a mandatory mainstream placement until the issues become acute, at which time the school is unable to cope, a lengthy process follows, parents are left fighting a battle to get the right provision and the child is faced with frustration, rejection and change. Society makes basic assumptions about child development, appropriate behaviour and social expectations, and when faced with children and young people who do not fit these stereotypes, many are quick to criticise and reject.

At times, parents describe everything as a battle, too often leading to consequences that overwhelm. Over and over again, parents have poured out their hearts about having to repeat their story, family history and needs at each new appointment with each new professional, be it health, education or social care. Anxiety and fatigue take over. Many families find that at least one parent has to give up their career to have the energy, strength and time to navigate the systems that are meant to be there to help. The economic and emotional consequences often seem to go unrecognised.

So many questions are asked:

- What does autism mean?
- How will we know how to help our child?
- Will they have friends?
- What does the future hold?
- Who will help us?
- Will our family and friends understand?
- Will I have to give up my job?

Everything seems overwhelming and the way ahead can look daunting. One parent was in a shop when her son became distressed. Another customer became verbally critical and reduced the mother to tears. Sharing her experience with the school her son attended resulted in the development of an autism awareness card to be provided for parents and staff to give to members of the public when difficult situations arose. This often changed disapproving looks and criticism to understanding. It is one of many ways in which to help raise community awareness and gradually increase understanding.

Add to this the fear that a child with autism often experiences in new situations that makes trips to the doctor, dentist, optician and shops highly charged and require meticulous planning. Consider the information in previous chapters about the frustrations related to communication, social understanding, resistance to change and sensory processing. When they are recognised as the backdrop to necessary appointments, the levels of anxiety are better understood. A benefit of getting to know other parents who share these issues is the network that can provide information on professionals who have a clear understanding of autism and plan for successful care. This was the case with a dentist who recognised the need for a first appointment for Mitch that was used purely to familiarise him with the setting: he could sit in the chair without any intervention, be shown the various instruments, hold a favourite toy and enjoy the chair going up and down, the air being used to tickle, etc. The appointment for the examination then went well, with Mitch casually entering the surgery and the treatment room.

Things don't always go so well, as was the case with Rena, who had an appointment at the local hospital for an EEG (electroencephalogram) after suspected epilepsy (approximately 30 per cent of individuals with autism are diagnosed with epilepsy). In spite of information being provided about Rena's needs, no preparation had been made to streamline the process or provide a quiet place to wait and administer the oral sedative. In the end, the appointment had to be abandoned – a traumatic situation for Rena and her father, making the rearranged appointment even more anxiety-inducing. There are occasions when children require a trip to the local hospital. Some schools work with their local A&E department to inform them of the needs of the pupils and encourage them to respond with sensitivity and understanding. By ringing ahead to forewarn that a child is coming to the department, the medical staff have the best opportunity to ensure that a cubicle is ready, to avoid the busy and distracting waiting room. Such adjustments should be the rule rather than the exception. Families should not be overwhelmed with anxiety when having to respond to the needs of their children.

Families also face the anxiety of planning a holiday, both at home and abroad – finding the right accommodation, recognising the issues around change but longing to have a change of scenery. The stress can be heightened when a flight is involved, and for families who have relatives abroad there is a need to foster these relationships. One such family asked their son's school for advice. This resulted in a letter to the airline from the school, outlining the family's concern and asking for understanding. It was well received and in response they enabled the family to be boarded last to reduce waiting time, seated them near the entry to the aircraft, heated the food that the family provided and were attentive throughout the flight. It always pays to ask for support.

Neighbours of families with children with autism can be supportive and helpful but, sadly, this is not always the case. One family reported having constant complaints because Oliver made exuberant noises when he was on the trampoline in the back garden. The comments were hurtful and the stress on the family took a toll on them. No one should have to live under a sense of oppression and criticism in their own home because they have a child with a disability. Community awareness is crucial for individuals with autism, their families and friends, in order to be genuinely accepted and given their full place in society.

Choosing a school

One of the most anxious times for families is discerning the right school context for their child. Getting it right at the Foundation Stage, enabling a strong, consistent start on which to build, is the goal for all. As mentioned, education authorities have long held the ideal that children should be educated in the 'least restrictive' environment. That is part of the philosophy of inclusion, providing the opportunity for all children to be educated in their local mainstream school. For some families of children with special educational needs this has been a positive experience, enabling both learning and social opportunities. For others, unfortunately, the lack of specialist understanding, inadequate staff training, inappropriate physical facilities and an unsympathetic ethos have proven to make success impossible. Placements breaking down, the search for a new and appropriate school, transition fears and the anxiety of starting, yet again, take a huge toll on both the child and the family. It is worth noting that while some parents fight for a specialist school, others fight just as hard to have their child in a mainstream school. Parental opinions are to be respected and when situations disappoint, the need for flexibility is essential.

It is no wonder that parents and carers feel alone and isolated when school experiences become negative. Too often special schools have to help pick up the pieces when a child in a mainstream setting has been excluded, sometimes on multiple occasions. Other children on the spectrum, not coping with the stress and lack of support, react through anger and outbursts from frustration or simply opt out completely. Many families relate stories about their child being sent home from school regularly. In one situation, Lionel's mother sat by the phone waiting and, inevitably, by 10.00 am, the phone rang with a message to say that they could not control her son and she was summoned to come to school to take him home. Is this inclusive education? Other parents report being asked to keep their child home when Ofsted was coming to review the school, or their child being excluded from school concerts, social activities and events. One family received a letter asking them to keep their son at home when the school was having a teddy bears' picnic because he wouldn't cope. Is this inclusion? Meg was being taught by a teaching assistant one to one in the corridor. Her parents were instructed to bring her to school just after the school day began, take her home for lunch and collect her at the end of the day before her peers left. Consequently, she had no opportunities for socialisation at any point in the school day. Is this inclusive education?

With the above as a backdrop, it becomes so important to choose the *right* school. The menu is wide:

- mainstream
- resourced provision attached to a mainstream school
- special education school
- autism specialist school.

Key factors for success are:

- full and transparent communication between the home and school
- comprehensive assessments that outline specific needs
- recognition of strengths as well as areas of difficulty
- the school's understanding of autism and the interventions to best support
- detailed individual planning and monitoring
- seamless and consistent support from all members of the school community.

As mentioned previously, many pupils have had negative experiences and the stress for both the child and the family was overwhelming. When moving to an appropriate school setting, one parent described the care, respect, sensitive support and cooperative work between home and school as a lifeline. Another commented that the staff 'make me feel safe and secure' and another that 'the teacher–parent barrier isn't there – there is good humour and warmth.' In this particular school context, the commitment of the school was also evidenced in the ongoing development of robust documentation, the ethos of the school and the positive relationships that were developed between students and staff. This was also echoed by a spontaneous email to the school from a parent who spoke of the changes in the child over the year, stating, 'He is growing into a beautiful boy and I couldn't be more proud. I want to say a huge thank you to all the staff that have helped him! You're all amazing! Thank you so much!'

Another parent expressed her absolute faith in the school that her teenager was attending. She praised all the staff and her son's class teacher in particular. She stated that her son had made so much progress that he was now able to enjoy life. When she was experiencing problems at home with her son, staff from school came out to help her and everything was sorted out. She said that she did not know how she would have coped without such tremendous support.

These examples show what is possible when the right context is found. The challenge and frustration is that the journey to get there is often fraught with difficulties and takes a toll on the health and wellbeing of both the autistic individual and their family.

Added extras

The good news is that there is an increasing number of schools where commitment is moving practice forward and recognising the needs of the whole child and the wider family. Some of the innovative programmes are described below.

The appointment of a parent advocate or family liaison officer can enable ease of communication, facilitate the support for consistency between home and school and help joined-up problem-solving as issues arise. This may also enable the development of a parent and carer support group, where relationships can be developed as mutual concerns are shared and where relevant topics are addressed, with guest speakers sometimes invited. Signposting parents to local amenities that support individuals with autism and helping them to navigate the myriad of forms to be completed for education, health and social care can be a godsend. Coffee mornings can also bring parents together and offer much-needed time for relaxation and conversation in a setting where they know that they are understood. Parents often report that these opportunities help them to feel less alone, knowing that others face similar challenges. One school appointed a Parent Ambassador as an innovative and positive role. The ambassador provides liaison between home and school, offers advice to parents, signposts to other agencies and generally responds to family and carer needs. As a parent of a child in the school, she is a true ambassador for ensuring that families and carers are well supported. The termly newsletter in one school was seen as more than school news – it was a professionally produced magazine with a wealth of information for parents and activity sheets for children. The Parent Ambassador worked with staff to 'translate' policies and other information into a user-friendly format. For example, the positive behaviour policy was rewritten into 'user-friendly' language and succinct presentation, accompanied by a full-page chart looking at observed behaviours and examples of positive language – for example, 'Feet on floor' to replace 'Stop climbing'. The magazine explained what the school improvement plan was and outlined the priorities. It provided a calendar of events, introduced new staff photographically, highlighted an individual class and what they had been doing and signposted parents to other local support – what a bonus for families and carers.

Involving parents in the life of the school can be done through, for example, participating in events, volunteering, being part of a working group for planning fundraising and being included through surveys on the positive and negative aspects of school life. The term 'parents as partners' is often used but going a step further, and accepting parents as 'critical friends' and inviting their ideas, creates a united school ethos that benefits all.

Going beyond the call of duty to offer opportunities after school, and play schemes on Saturdays and during holiday breaks, is highly beneficial. One school had a monthly games session that included a light meal and choice of activities suited to individuals. Social opportunities, communication and widening experiences were all part of the agenda. The young people, many of whom had few friends and activities outside of school, loved this time of relaxation. The added benefit – and part of the *raison d'être* – was to provide an opportunity for siblings to have uninterrupted time with their parents, relax, go out for a meal, etc. The family reaction to this activity was 100 per cent positive.

Summer play schemes to provide some well-organised and structured activities to break up the long holiday are also beneficial to children and young people and their parents and carers. Many schools recognise the value of this in their planning, with staff known to the children volunteering to lead and be involved in sessions. This also creates continuity, which prevents children from being away from school for so long that the start of the new term is traumatic.

Residential breaks require extensive planning and risk assessment and yet are often organised for the added benefit of children and their families. The opportunities provided include development of independence, new experiences, physical activities and social bonding. Many students and parents recognise the positive impact of the familiar (school staff and peers) being consistent while the unfamiliar (venue, change in routine and diverse surroundings) is introduced and embraced.

Within a supportive and committed school environment, the whole child and the full gambit of life are addressed and creatively planned for. School photographs can be a nightmare – but not when a photographer is willing to throw himself into taking photos in any situation with any background until he 'catches' the right one that celebrates each child. Toilet training and personal hygiene can be so complex and frightening until a problem-solving member of staff works with the family to find the way forward to change quality of life. Getting out together as a family can seem impossible until the school hosts a summer picnic or barbecue in the secure setting of the school playground, where everyone can relax and enjoy eating and socialising together. One school planned a camping weekend for families to have this experience in the safety of the school's grounds, where they and their children could be themselves and experience new things. For some families this was a 'trial run', leading to camping further afield.

In another school, an assembly highlighted the family of one child. This has been an ongoing theme, with each pupil having the opportunity to showcase their family to the others. The families were asked to provide photographs and information and, over time, these have been added to a display board in the shared area for all to see. With minimal support, this pupil showed his poster of the family and answered questions from his peers. From a very early age, children in this school are encouraged to be presenters and to listen and respond to each other through their own communication mode.

Sibling support

Having a brother or sister on the autism spectrum can be confusing for siblings. Some describe a feeling of isolation and embarrassment, or worry about bringing friends home because of the unique behaviour of their sibling. Some describe feelings of confusion because they just don't understand the complexity of what they experience. Some describe being resentful because the autistic sibling seems to get the lion's share of attention from their parents. Some describe anger because their sibling disregards their personal space and destroys their possessions. All of these feelings are valid and should not be dismissed. They need sensitive understanding and support.

There are some amazing siblings, mature beyond their years, who determine to be understanding and protective, who encourage, celebrate and foster progress very naturally. Recognising the frustrations and the obstacles that the family have faced in getting the right support, some of these young people have committed to pursuing careers that will make life better for families and individuals where autism is identified. Speech and language therapy, occupational therapy, psychology, mental health and educational roles providing understanding are undertaken with a view to serving, to being part of the solution.

Staff qualities are very important and an ongoing theme has been the importance of creativity. One teacher hired by a specialist autism school was, on paper, not the strongest candidate. She was young, a newly qualified teacher. During the interview she was asked why she felt that a role in such a unique environment was right for her. She explained her background as a triplet with one sister having special needs. She accompanied her sister to a summer play scheme where she was asked to befriend a child on the autism spectrum. From this young age, this encounter sparked her interest and she did not lose sight of this through the years ahead. While in sixth form she volunteered with children with autism, her dissertation was focused on autism and she then worked in a residential provision for further experience. Only then did she apply for this teaching position. The job was offered and accepted with enthusiasm. The qualities of this young woman were an asset to the team: enthusiasm, absolute commitment to her pupils and the families that they represented, and never being faced with a problem without searching for a creative solution.

Recognising the issues faced by siblings and offering support is essential and can be life-changing. One approach is to host sibling workshops where they are invited to come together to get to know each other and to explore an understanding of autism. One activity used a large outline of the human body on the floor, with each sibling given sticky notes to write attributes related to their brother or sister and place them on the body form. For example, kicking went on the feet and hair-pulling on the head. When the activity was complete there was such a wide-eyed response – so many had not realised that their experiences were shared by others. The sharing of stories and the coping strategies that they employed created a buzz in the room. New friends were made, and a new understanding, acceptance and confidence were clearly evident.

During summer, play schemes were organised, offering activities for students and providing some family respite over the summer break. Some sibling days were also organised, when they would have opportunities to learn more about autism and spend some time with their brothers and sisters – or have a break from them! Lunchtime was an opportunity to choose, and it is interesting to note that every participant chose to sit and engage with their sibling. There was a real sense of pride in being part of the family group.

On one occasion, an early evening workshop was offered for parents, with a parallel session for siblings running in another part of the school. This was one of the few times that negative responses were forthcoming. Both sessions began with the invitation for the parents and siblings to say something positive about their family member. One parent hesitated and said, 'I can't think of anything good to say.' In the session running concurrently, the children of the same family also lacked any positive comments – very sad and troubling. All children have positive attributes that need to be celebrated and we all blossom when they are accentuated. The evening's discussion, sharing enthusiasm about small steps of progress and creative approaches to challenges, helped this family to recognise potential and the importance of embracing and affirming the contribution that each member of the family makes.

While it is sometimes difficult for families to feel comfortable with letting others into their lives, the understanding and encouragement of others including peers, to both parents and children, is so important. Some families get to know others through school events, forming family friendships and mutual support. Some book holidays together, knowing that taking turns with childcare means more quality time for all. For siblings, to have their peers in the home, to raise awareness and know that their frustrations are understood, is healthy for their wellbeing.

Tip

Many parents have shared their stories about how they and their nuclear and extended families have been supported by committed professionals in schools, social care and community structures. Wouldn't it be wonderful if this was always the case? Where opportunities are provided and support is given for issues of concern, families gain confidence in the 'system' and see light at the end of the tunnel.

Transitions

The importance of planning for both micro- and macro-transitions has been addressed in Chapter 3. When change and new experiences cause anxiety, and often rejection, it is imperative that planning is undertaken with care.

Transitions include moving from home to school, from class to class, from primary to secondary, and leading to what comes next. College? Employment? Negotiating what the obstacles will be, what support will be provided and what new hurdles will need to be overcome is all part of the burden of responsibility faced by parents of children with autism. Aspirations for relevant and meaningful opportunities, acceptance and affirmation, and the confidence to know that your child at any age is having fulfilment in life, are longed for.

Parents of autistic children in the Early Years are already asking themselves, 'What will happen when we're gone?' There is worry about long-term care, others who will value and nurture the child, and the child becoming an adult who is unable to cope without support. For some, siblings grow up accepting this role as a joy because it is based on love. Other siblings, who love no less, fear that this role will limit their own opportunities for independence and adventure. The underlying anxiety and worry that looking to the future causes is something that parents of neurotypical families seldom face, as they expect their children to mature and progress into independence with minimal pitfalls along the journey.

Thankfully, many examples of 'going the second mile' are observed in education and care provisions. For example, one parent explained that her son finished college with no prospects of employment, causing distress for both parents and their adolescent son. She glowed when she explained that she chatted with his former school, and the deputy head, knowing that her son loved gardening, organised a placement at a local garden centre that then became a regular job – the second mile.

Future concerns

One of the common threads of parents' conversations is that they meet the same obstacles at every new junction – starting school, moving from stage to stage, to college, to university to employment. The journey does not seem to become smoother.

The previous chapter of this book detailed statistics about employment and mental health. Even highly educated individuals on the autism spectrum find it challenging to find relevant employment. We recognise the frustration faced by so many adults with autism who are disadvantaged in the workplace and whose strengths are not recognised. Schools offer support, colleges and universities offer support and then… misunderstanding and lack of awareness of reasonable adjustments often result in lack of opportunities or short-lived employment.

Creativity has been mentioned throughout this book and the creativity of parents cannot be overlooked. For example, a young man without an opportunity for work was supported by his family to begin an egg business. He loved the family's chickens and, by expanding their number and laying capacity, he was able to secure clients to whom he delivered eggs every week. It gave him the responsibility of managing the flock, collecting, cleaning and packing the eggs, keeping the records of delivery and payment, etc. How wonderful it would be if there was a community commitment to investing in work opportunities to support our young people and adults on the autism spectrum.

Ways forward

Community awareness is one of the keys to the future for individuals with autism and their families, carers and friends, and to achieving their proper place in society. There are now some employers who have proactively recognised the qualities of some individuals on the spectrum and value their skills in the workplace – thought patterns, attention to detail and work ethics that are common among people on the autism spectrum. Preferring routine, being focused on the task and not being prone to socialising during work all point to a strong work ethic.

Some local community organisations have sought to increase their understanding of autism to develop strategies and make inclusion not only possible but positive. Cinemas and supermarkets where an 'autism hour' has been provided, for instance, are showing awareness and support and setting an example to the wider community. Some galleries and museums have developed user-friendly guides to make visits less stressful. On a more individual basis, many families speak of local cafés and shops who have got to know the family and now make them welcome, often being flexible in their service.

We have a dream that someday there will be full understanding, acceptance and inclusion of individuals of all ages who have a diagnosis of autism. A dream that each will be given the respect and value that is deserved. A dream that every family will be well supported, and have confidence in the education, social care and health opportunities provided for their children from cradle to grave. We have a dream that communities will be welcoming and value the positive aspects of autism, and welcome and enable employment that is not tokenistic but is relevant and fulfilling. **We have a dream!**

Family takeaways

- Always have high expectations.
- Advocate for your child and others.
- Celebrate each milestone.
- Recognise the strengths that your child brings to the family.
- Find ways to increase the understanding of autism in your wider family and circle of friends.
- Seek out the most appropriate school setting.
- Expect support for transitions at every stage of development.
- Encourage employers to make reasonable adjustments to enable successful job opportunities.
- Access support through appropriate training opportunities.
- Raise community awareness.

Glossary

Alert cards: Credit-card-sized identification provided by various autism organisations and many police forces to help communicate the needs of autistic/ neurodivergent individuals, to tell people about the condition and to ask them to show respect.

Alert Program: A user-friendly approach, helping individuals to articulate their self-regulation or alertness. Simple strategies are outlined in the *Take Five!* book (available at www.alertprogram.com/product/take-five-staying-alert-at-home-and-school).

Ambitious about Autism: A national charity for children and young people with autism, providing services, raising awareness and campaigning for change.

Asperger syndrome: One of a group of neurodevelopmental disorders. It was formerly characterised as a distinct autism spectrum disorder, but the *DSM-5* in May 2013 combined the diagnosis with autistic disorder into one condition called autism spectrum disorder, or ASD.

Attention Autism: An intervention model designed by Gina Davies, specialist speech and language therapist. It aims to develop natural and spontaneous communication through the use of visually based and highly motivating activities.

Attention deficit disorder (ADD): A neurological disorder that causes a range of problems, such as difficulty in attending to instruction, focusing on schoolwork, keeping up with assignments, following instructions, completing tasks and social interaction.

Autism: A lifelong developmental disorder that affects how people communicate and interact with the world. Treatments and services can improve a person's symptoms and ability to function.

Autism Champions (sometimes called ambassadors): Individuals who share an interest in autism and a passion to raise awareness and understanding.

Autism Diagnostic Interview: A structured interview conducted with the parents of individuals who have been referred for the evaluation of possible autism or autism spectrum disorders.

Autism spectrum disorder: Autism is known as a 'spectrum' disorder because there is wide variation in the type and severity of symptoms that people experience. ASD occurs in all ethnic, racial and economic groups.

BIGmack: A simple communication device used to record speech, music, etc., enabling the user to play it back at the appropriate time by pressing a button.

Central coherence: The term given to the ability to see overall meaning from numerous details. It is the difference between seeing a forest rather than the individual trees.

Child and Adolescent Mental Health Services (CAMHS): The name for the NHS services that assess and treat young people with emotional, behavioural or mental health difficulties.

DSM: *The Diagnostic and Statistical Manual of Mental Disorders.*

Dysregulation: The inability to manage the intensity and duration of negative emotions such as fear, sadness or anger.

Echolalia: The repetition of a word or phrase just spoken by another person.

Education health and care plan (EHCP): An outline of any special educational needs that a child has and the provision that a local authority must put in place to help them.

Executive function: The mental processes that enable us to plan, focus attention, recall instructions and deal with multiple tasks.

Forest School: An outdoor education delivery model in which students visit natural spaces to learn personal, social and technical skills.

Functional analysis: This determines the reason and purpose for a behaviour, identifying triggers such as context, time of day, individuals involved, level of expectations, etc.

Gloop: A mixture of cornflour and water used for exploratory sensory play.

Hanen Centre: A not-for-profit charitable organisation committed to promoting language, social and literacy skills in young children.

Hypersensitive: Being oversensitive to particular things in the environment.

Hyposensitive: Having an abnormally decreased sensitivity to sensory input.

Inclusion: The practice or policy of providing equal access to opportunities and resources for people who might otherwise be excluded or marginalised, including education, employment and community services.

Intensive interaction: A practical approach to interacting with people with learning disabilities who struggle with communicating or being social, by providing a communication partner with whom to form relationships.

Interoception: A sense that provides information about the internal condition of our bodies, allowing the experience of many bodily sensations, such as a growling stomach, thirst, tense muscles or a racing heartbeat.

Kanner, Leo: An Austrian-American psychiatrist referred to as the 'father of child psychiatry' in the United States. He is considered the first scientist to diagnose autism in 1943.

Mindfulness: A type of meditation focusing on being intensely aware of what you're sensing and feeling in the moment. It involves breathing methods, guided imagery and other practices to foster relaxation and reduce stress.

NAS EarlyBird: A programme for parents and carers to support autistic children under five years old. It helps them to understand their child's autism, enter their child's world, make contact and find ways to develop interaction, communication and understand their child's behaviour.

National Autistic Society (NAS): The UK's leading charity for people on the autism spectrum and their families, providing support, guidance and advice, as well as campaigning for improved rights, services and opportunities to help create a society that works for autistic people.

Neurodiversity: Refers to variation in the human brain regarding sociability, learning, attention, mood and other mental functions.

Neurotypicals (NT): An abbreviation of 'neurologically typical', widely used in the autistic community as a label for people who are born without a developmental disability.

NICE (National Institute of Health and Care Excellence): Guidelines covering diagnosing and managing suspected or confirmed autism spectrum disorder (autism, Asperger syndrome and atypical autism) in people aged 18 and over. It aims to improve access and engagement with interventions and services, and to improve the experience of care for people with autism.

Obsessive compulsive disorder (OCD): A disorder in which a person has repetitive thoughts (obsessions) or the need to perform routines repeatedly (compulsions), to an extent that generates distress or impairs general functioning.

Pathological demand avoidance (PDA): A profile that describes those whose main characteristic is to avoid everyday demands and expectations to an extreme extent. It is distinct from autism but falls under the spectrum.

Pica: An eating disorder that involves compulsively eating items that have no nutritional value, such as dirt, hair, paper, string, etc.

Picture Exchange Communication System (PECS)®: A type of augmentative and alternative communication that uses visual symbols to teach the learner to communicate with parents, carers, teachers and peers. The aim is to teach intentional, functional communication and to allow users to communicate their wants and needs.

Proprioception: The sense through which we perceive the position and movement of our bodies, including our sense of equilibrium and balance, senses that depend on the notion of force.

Restraint collapse: After a child tries to maintain a certain level of energy, mental motivation, emotional containment and physical control while at school, they are able to express themselves without fear of judgement or consequences when they arrive home.

SCERTS® (Social Communication, Emotional Regulation and Transactional Support): A research-based educational approach and multidisciplinary framework that directly addresses the core challenges faced by children and persons with ASD and related disabilities and their families. The model builds on competence in social communication, emotional regulation and transactional support and is applicable for individuals with a wide range of abilities and ages across home, school and community settings.

Self-injurious behaviours (SIB): This refers to when someone intentionally damages or injures their body. Typically, it is a way of attempting to cope with emotional distress or respond to anxiety when it is impossible to communicate feelings in other ways.

Sensory circuit: A short sequence of activities carried out repeatedly to provide the child with the right type of sensory input in order to calm and organise them for the day ahead, ready for learning to occur.

Sensory diet: An intervention treatment that supports children with sensory processing issues. It includes a series of physical and sensory activities. An occupational therapist can design a sensory diet routine tailored to meet individual needs.

Sensory resources: A range of equipment, from stress balls to platform swings, that is used to calm or stimulate and support sensory regulation.

Social Stories™: Narratives made to illustrate particular situations and problems and how people deal with them. They help children with autism to understand social norms and to learn how to communicate with others appropriately. The Social Stories™ concept was developed by child paediatrician Dr Carol Gray.

Special educational needs and disabilities (SEND): A UK government code of practice that defines special educational needs and explains what will be provided to meet identified need.

SPELL: Developed by the National Autistic Society, this is a framework for understanding and responding to the needs of children and adults on the autism spectrum, developed through evidence-based practice.

Teaching and Education of Autistic and Related Communication Handicapped Children (TEACCH): A method of structured teaching based on the unique learning needs and strengths of people with ASD, including visual information processing.

Transition: This refers to times of change, ranging from micro changes, such as the minor changes experienced each day, to macro changes, such as a new school, a new year group, a new job or a new home.

Unstructured time: This refers to the times in the day that are not clearly structured, such as breaks, social times, holidays, etc.

Vestibular: The sensory system contributing to the sense of balance and spatial orientation for coordinating balance and movement.

Further reading and useful resources

Books

The Reason I Jump: One boy's voice from the silence of autism by Naoki Higashida and David Mitchell (2014, Spectre Publishing)
A really powerful personal account (translated by David Mitchell) in a useful and accessible question-and-answer format.

Fall Down Seven Times, Get Up Eight: A young man's voice from the silence of autism by Naoki Higashida and David Mitchell (2018, Spectre Publishing)
The follow-up to *The Reason I Jump* from a young adult's perspective.

Thinking in Pictures by Temple Grandin (2006, Bloomsbury)
Dr Temple Grandin is a very well-respected animal scientist who is autistic. This book is about her childhood, labelled as severely autistic, and it really is a must-read. Many of Temple Grandin's books give a very powerful insight into autism, the 'autistic brain' and life with autism.
Other books by Temple Grandin: *The Autistic Brain* (2014), *The Way I See It* (5th edition, 2020) and *Different Not Less* (2nd edition, 2020) – all Future Publishing

Nobody Nowhere: The remarkable autobiography of an autistic girl by Donna Williams (1998, Jessica Kingsley Publishers)
A remarkable and challenging book. Diagnosed at 25, following years of being labelled many, many times, Donna Williams came across autism and it all made sense. This book presents the view from the autism world. Donna Williams has written many books on autism, and her four autobiographies give an insight into the world of autism.
Other books by Donna Williams: *Somebody Somewhere* (1998), *Like Colour to the Blind* (1999) and *Everyday Heaven* (2004) – all Jessica Kingsley Publishers

The Complete Guide to Asperger's Syndrome by Tony Attwood (2006, Jessica Kingsley Publishers)

Dr Tony Attwood is a world-renowned 'expert' on Asperger syndrome. This is perhaps the definitive book on the syndrome and a must-have for all who are affected by Asperger's in any way.

Dr Attwood's earlier book, *Asperger's Syndrome: A guide for parents and professionals*, was published in 1997 but is nonetheless a very useful read.

NeuroTribes: The legacy of autism and how to think smarter about people who think differently by Steve Silberman (2015, Allen & Unwin)

A thought-provoking and very readable book about autism, its history and the part that it plays in enriching the human experience.

Sensory Perceptual Issues in Autism and Asperger Syndrome by Olga Bogdashina (2016, Jessica Kingsley Publishers)

A very interesting read, which addresses the sensory issues that people with autism encounter. The book includes some very practical suggestions to mitigate the difficulties.

Theory of Mind and the Triad of Perspectives on Autism and Asperger Syndrome by Olga Bogdashina (2005, Jessica Kingsley Publishers)

Written from the perspective of a mother of a child with autism, the book provides a wealth of information on different thinking and 'mindblindness' – a lack of 'theory of mind'.

A Girl Like Tilly: Growing up with autism by Helen Bates and Ellen Li (2016, Jessica Kingsley Publishers)

For children in primary schools, this book tells the story of an able girl and her difficulties with thinking differently and struggling with her differences. Very poignant.

100 Ideas for Supporting Pupils on the Autistic Spectrum by Francine Brower (2007, Bloomsbury)

A really useful and practical guide for teachers and anyone working with children with autism.

100 Ideas for Primary Teachers: Supporting pupils with autism by Francine Brower (2019, Bloomsbury)

A companion volume to the above title, full of very practical suggestions based on a wealth of experience in the field.

People with Autism Behaving Badly: Helping people with ASD move on from behavioural and emotional challenge by John Clements (2005, Jessica Kingsley Publishers)

A really excellent book, written in an easily accessible format for parents and teachers. Full of very practical ideas, free from jargon and grounded in knowledge and experience.

Behavioural Concerns and Autism Spectrum Disorders by Ewa Zarkowska and John Clements (2000, Jessica Kingsley Publishers)

Another really good book that addresses many common behavioural difficulties encountered by people on the autism spectrum.

Autism and Asperger Syndrome in Adults by Dr Luke Beardon (2016, Sheldon Press)

Recommended for families living with autism, adults going through diagnosis and all professionals working in the field. This is a must-read book.

10 Things Every Child with Autism Wishes You Knew by Ellen Notbohm (2019, Future Horizon)

Written by a mother of sons with autism and ADHD, this is a very grounded and practical volume – perhaps most useful for parents of newly diagnosed children.

Working with Girls and Young Women on the Autism Spectrum by Fiona Bullivant (2018, Jessica Kingsley Publishers)

There is a real shortage of books about the female experience of autism, and it is particularly helpful to hear the voices of autistic girls themselves.

Books on autism for children

My Awesome Autism: Helping children learn about their autism diagnosis by Nikki Saunders (2019, independently published)

He's Not Naughty! A children's guide to autism by Deborah Brownson (2019, Jessica Kingsley Publishers)

The Superhero Brain: Explaining autism to empower kids by Christel Land (2017, CreateSpace Independent Publishing Platform)

Different Like Me: My book of autism heroes by Jennifer Elder (2005, Jessica Kingsley Publishers)

All Cats are on the Autism Spectrum by Kathy Hoopmann (2020, Jessica Kingsley Publishers)

Websites

There are millions of websites about autism, but not all of them are either useful or appropriate. When searching for information on the subject, a great deal of discrimination is needed – approach with caution and eyes wide open!

National Autistic Society: www.autism.org.uk

Autism Alliance: www.autism-alliance.org.uk

Scottish Autism: www.scottishautism.org

Autism Wales: www.apcymru.org.uk

Ambitious about Autism: www.ambitiousaboutautism.org.uk

Approaches and interventions

There is no definitive intervention; no one approach or intervention is 100 per cent effective for 100 per cent of people with autism, 100 per cent of the time. When investigating approaches and interventions, objectivity and open eyes are a must. There are many 'snake oil salesmen' in the field of autism. The authors have well over 60 years of working in the field of autism, and we do not advocate any single approach or intervention. Our experience would suggest that an eclectic, individualistic approach is often the most effective.

EarlyBird and Hanen – More Than Words

The EarlyBird programme has been developed by the National Autistic Society to empower and support parents and carers of young children with a diagnosis of autism. The programme aims to help:

- understand your child's autism
- structure interactions to develop communication
- develop strategies to pre-empt problem behaviours and/or manage those behaviours that are already causing problems.

The 'More Than Words' programme was designed specifically for parents of children aged five and under with autism and with other social communication difficulties. Addressing the unique needs of these children, the programme aims to provide parents with the tools, strategies and support that they may need to help their children to communicate. More Than Words aims to do this by empowering parents and carers to help the child reach the following three goals:

1. improved social communication and back-and-forth interactions

2. improved play skills

3. improved imitation skills.

Schools across the country often provide the More Than Words sessions, and the EarlyBird programme is provided by the NHS, local authority or appropriate autism charities in your region.

Applied behaviour analysis

Applied behaviour analysis (ABA) refers to interventions that are developed from a branch of science called behaviour analysis. A claimed strength of ABA for children with autism is that it addresses behaviour relevant to that child (both excesses and deficits). ABA programmes are claimed to be very different from those 20 years ago. Like all interventions for autism, ABA is not for everyone; it does not 'cure' the condition, but it has a place in adapting behaviours. There are several organisations that are strong proponents of the approach, such as Ambitious about Autism and Child Autism UK, for example. Discrete trial training is very similar to ABA approaches but tends to focus on a very specific skill to learn or behaviour to reduce.

TEACCH (Treatment and Education of Autistic and Communication Handicapped Children)

Developed in North Carolina in the 1970s, supporters of TEACCH see the approach as a lifelong one that focuses on the individual and their strengths, their interests and their needs. Understanding autism and the 'culture of autism' is very important. Structured teaching, developing routines and clarity of communication are fundamental. Many successful schools and services adapt elements of TEACCH to work with both children and adults with autism. Further information can be found at Autism Independent UK (autismuk.com) and the National Autistic Society (autism.org.uk).

PECS (Picture Exchange Communication System)®

Developed by speech therapists to encourage expressive language, allowing the person to express needs, wants and emotions, etc., PECS® is an evidence-based functional communication system. PECS® is most effective at an early stage and the major drawback is that it requires a speech and language therapist to implement the programmes.

SCERTS® (Social Communication/Emotional Regulation/ Transactional Support)

The SCERTS® model is an educational model developed in the USA by occupational and speech therapists. It was developed to help families, educators and therapists work cooperatively together in supporting the child. The major drawback is that it is incredibly difficult to follow the programmes in a typical school setting (either mainstream or special school). The acronym refers to the focus on: social communication (SC) – the development of functional communication and emotional expression; emotional regulation (ER) – the development of well-regulated emotions and the ability to cope with stress; and transactional support (TS) – the implementation of support to help families, teachers and therapists respond to children's needs, adapt the environment and provide tools to enable learning. Many autism-specific schools have adapted elements of SCERTS®.

Son-Rise

This programme is a home-based approach which claims to develop the relationship between parents and child. The parents are seen as key therapists, through 'joining' the child in their world. There is no independent evidence to support this approach; however, many parents anecdotally feel that the interventions have improved the parent–child relationship.

Sensory integration

It is now recognised that sensory processing is a significant element of the autism jigsaw. Sensory integration claims to help people with autism to organise their responses to sensory sensations, both internally and externally. Specially trained occupational therapists are needed to devise and implement the programmes, which are initially required to be undertaken in a specialist therapy room. As yet, there is no firm scientific evidence for SI therapy; however, again anecdotally, the use of specific interventions (weighted vests, for example) has been seen to aid focus and attention.

There are other approaches and interventions advertised or promoted across the internet. However, a very healthy dose of scepticism and caution is advised – some interventions are detrimental. Quite understandably, many parents are looking for help with the condition and can be vulnerable to alternative, unregulated, unresearched and unethical treatments. *But autism is a difference, not a disease.*

References

All Party Parliamentary Group on Autism (APPGA) and the National Autistic Society (2019), 'The *Autism Act*, 10 Years On', https://pearsfoundation.org.uk/wp-content/uploads/2019/09/APPGA-Autism-Act-Inquiry-Report.pdf

Ambitious about Autism (2018), 'We need an education', www.ambitiousaboutautism.org.uk/sites/default/files/resources-and-downloads/files/we-need-an-education-exclusions-report.pdf

American Psychiatric Association (2013), *Diagnostic and Statistical Manual of Mental Disorders* (5th edn.). Arlington, VA: American Psychiatric Association.

Autism Speaks (undated), 'Autism statistics and facts', www.autismspeaks.org/autism-statistics-asd

BBC Radio 4 (2020), 'Broad spectrum', www.bbc.co.uk/programmes/m000mcyj

Bogdashina, O. (2003), *Sensory Perceptual Issues in Autism and Asperger Syndrome*. London: Jessica Kingsley Publishers.

Brown, M. (1986), *Arthur's Teacher Trouble*. New York, NY: Little, Brown and Company.

Clements, J. and Zarkowska, E. (2000), *Behavioural Concerns and Autistic Spectrum Disorders: Explanations and strategies for change*. London: Jessica Kingsley Publishers.

Grandin, T. (2006), *Thinking in Pictures* (2nd edn.). London: Bloomsbury.

Grandin, T. (2009), 'Temple Grandin on "The Best Life For Animals"', www.npr.org/templates/story/story.php?storyId=99009110&t=1613656027516

Hepworth, D. (2017), 'A critical review of current police training and policy for autism spectrum disorder', *Journal of Intellectual Disabilities and Offending Behaviour*, 8, (4), 212–222.

Hill, A. P., Zuckerman, K. E., Hagen, A. D., Kriz, D. J., Duvall, S. W., van Santen, J., Nigg, J., Fair, D. and Fombonne, E. (2014), 'Aggressive behavior problems in children with autism spectrum disorders: Prevalence and correlates in a large clinical sample', *Research in Autism Spectrum Disorders*, 8, (9), 1121–1133.

Knapp, M., Romeo, R. and Beecham, J. (2009), 'Economic cost of autism in the UK', *Autism*, 13, (3), 317–336.

Loomes, R., Hull, L. and Mandy, W. P. L. (2017), 'What is the male-to-female ratio in autism spectrum disorder? A systematic review and meta-analysis', *American Journal of Child and Adolescent Psychiatry*, 56, (6), 466–474.

NASEN (2016), 'Girls and autism: Flying under the radar', https://nasen.org.uk/resources/girls-and-autism-flying-under-radar

National Autistic Society (undated), 'Autism and gender identity', www.autism.org.uk/advice-and-guidance/what-is-autism/autism-and-gender-identity

National Autistic Society (2014), 'Diverse perspectives', https://s3.chorus-mk.thirdlight. com/file/1573224908/63849355948/width=-1/height=-1/format=-1/fit=scale/ t=445333/e=never/k=7c17beeb/Diverse-perspectives-report.pdf

National Autistic Society (2016), 'The autism employment gap', www.autism.org.uk/ what-we-do/news/government-must-tackle-the-autism-employment-gap

National Autistic Society (2020), 'Self-injurious behaviour – a guide for all audiences', www.autism.org.uk/advice-and-guidance/topics/behaviour/self-injurious-behaviour/all-audiences

Raymond, J. (2010), 'Temple Grandin on her struggles and "yak yaks"', NBC News, www.nbcnews.com/health/health-news/temple-grandin-her-struggles-yak-yaks-flna1c9442451

Summers, J., Shahrami, A., Cali, S., D'Mello, C., Kako, M., Palikucin-Reljin, A., Savage, M., Shaw, O. and Lunsky, Y. (2017), 'Self-injury in autism spectrum disorder and intellectual disability: Exploring the role of reactivity to pain and sensory input', *Brain Sciences*, 7, (11), 140.

Taylor, B., Jick, H. and MacLaughlin, D. (2013), 'Prevalence and incidence rates of autism in the UK: Time trend from 2004–2010 in children aged 8 years', *BMJ Open*, 3:e003219.

UK Parliament (2020), Autism (POSTnote no. 612), https://post.parliament.uk/ research-briefings/post-pn-0612

Williams, D. (1998), *Nobody Nowhere: The remarkable autobiography of an autistic girl*. London: Jessica Kingsley Publishers.

Index